How to become Software Architect

Dedicated to my mother Meera Devi

Author information

For any help please contact :
Amazon Author Page :
amazon.com/author/ajaykumar
Email : ajaycucek@gmail.com ,
ajaxreso@gmail.com
Linkedin :
https://www.linkedin.com/in/ajaycucek
Facebook :
https://www.facebook.com/ajaycucek
Youtube :
https://www.youtube.com/channel/UC1uXE
ebtqCLYxVdzirKZGIA
Twitter : https://twitter.com/ajaycucek
Instagram :
https://www.instagram.com/ajaycucek/
Skype : ajaycucek

Table of contents

The Software Architect's Role in the Enterprise

Book Introduction

This book is for any developer that aspires to become an architect or any newly minted architect that needs some help getting started. There's lots of information and opinions on the practice of the software architect. So much so that it can be very confusing getting started. I remember a number of years ago when I decided it was time to move into the architect role. I wasn't really sure what to do. I was a senior developer and very comfortable in that role. I like designing software and leading a team and thought the next logical step would be to move into the architect role. While this was a great career move I wasn't fully aware how different the role would be. This is a very common experience in how most developer's transition to the role of the architect.

Course Overview

- **Fundamentals of being a software architect in the enterprise**

- The Who and What of Software Architecture
  - Who a software architect is
  - What the role entails
  - Skills, Knowledge & Duties
- Architects role in the project life cycle
  - Discuss each phase of the project life cycle
  - What effective architects do in each phase
- Design
  - Design process
  - How to effectively communicate your designs
- Practical as possible

In this book I'm going to cover the fundamentals of being a software architect in the enterprise. We're going to get started by discussing the Who and the What of software architecture. In the first module you'll learn who a software architect is and what his or her role entails in the enterprise. We'll talk about the skills, the knowledge, and the duties that an effective software architect should possess. In the second module we'll discuss the architect's role in the project life cycle. We'll discuss each phase in the project life cycle and outline specifically what effective architects do in each of these phases. In the third and fourth modules we'll focus solely on the design process and how to effectively communicate your design to both technical and non-technical stakeholders.

Overview

This module is The Who and What of Software Architecture. It's quite common for organizations to have software architects assigned to development teams or even have a group of architects on an architecture team, however the expectations of the people that occupy this role are often very unclear. The Who & What of Software Architecture

- Software Architect role in the organization is often not clearly defined
- Skills
- Knowledge
- Duties
- Who is a software architect?
- What is an architect expected to be skilled at?
- What is an architect expected to know?
- What is an architect expected to do?
    - Technical & Non-Technical
- Why does an organization need software architects?

The organization knows that they need someone with a development background to help design solutions and deliver projects but they often aren't able to identify what specifically the architect should be doing. In this module I'm going to do just that. I'm going to enumerate the skills, knowledge, and duties of the software architect. I'm going to begin by answering the following questions: Who is a software architect? What is an architect expected to be skilled at? What is an architect expected to know? And what is an architect expected to do, outlining both the technical and non-technical duties. Because most everyone taking this book comes from a development background I'm going to spend a bit more time covering the non-technical duties. These are the ones that most new architects struggle with. In the last section of this module I'll discuss why an organization needs software architects and provide a few practical examples. Now let's get started.

Who is an Architect?

Who is a Software Architect?
- Why are your applications in the state they are in?
- Silo'd design
- Little or no reuse
- Poor design
- Why?
- Same discussion over and over
- No time
- No resources
- Need to redesign...
- Redesign is difficult
- Talk but no action
- Design but no implementation
- Business doesn't see the benefit

Have you ever been in a meeting where you sit around with a handful of other developers discussing why your applications are in the state they're in? Why they're designed using such a Silo'd approach and why there's little reuse? Better yet have you ever asked yourself why an application was designed the way it was because it just makes no sense to you and for the life of you, you can't understand why someone would do that? Oftentimes we as developers find our self in meetings having the same discussion over and over again trying to figure out how we're going to get the time and resources to change an existing application to take a more modern approach to a design or to be more efficient or interoperable. We often wish we would've had these thoughts early on because it -- because to make these types of changes now is at best very difficult and at worse near impossible. Most often we just talk about making these changes but we never act. Sometimes we even design solutions to fix these problems but we never implement them because we just don't have the time or the business just doesn't see the benefit. In our heart we know this is the right thing to do but we just can't make the business case to move forward. I know many of you are shaking your heads in agreement right now. I've been developing software for many F years now and I can't tell you how many times I've sat in meetings with my fellow developers discussing this exact thing. It doesn't matter if you're in a large company or a three-man shop, this is our world. Software architect is the person or persons on your team that mitigates these types of challenges.

Who is a Software Architect?

The person with the skills, the knowledge, and the experience to address the challenges an application will encounter before, during, and after construction. This person may not have the architect title but we all know he or she has the best intentions of the development team, the business, and the application in mind. This person has the knowledge and skills to take a project from an abstract set of business goals to reality.

Who is a Software Architect?

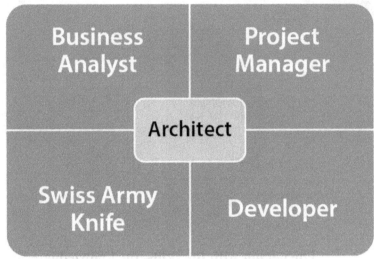

This person quite often can stand in for any role in the project from Business Analyst, Project Manager, to Developer. He or she is available to fill any gaps on the project no matter what skill is needed. This person is committed to the success of the project no matter what curves technical or otherwise are thrown at it. He or she is basically the Swiss army knife of the project. Wikipedia states that a software architect is "a computer programmer who makes high-level design choices and dictates technical standards, including software coding standards, tools, and platforms. " Generally this is true but those of us who have occupied this role know it's much more than this. I think a more realistic description of the role is used by Rebecca Grinter in her article titled Systems Architecture Product Designing and Social Engineering. In the article she describes the architect as not only a Master Technologist but a Master

Collaborator responsible not only for designing the solution but making sure the solution is accepted and supported by all groups in the organization. She says that "architects work in ways that allow them to accomplish their dual mission of designing technically possible and organizationally feasible products. They bring people from all over the corporation in to consult on their technical knowledge, and at the same time learn about their groups' priorities and schedules. The architects present their work to different groups to ensure that the solutions are attractive to build, buy, and sell. Finally, they continually look outside the company to align their work with standards agencies and competitors. All of this is necessary design work, without it, solutions might work, but could not be built or sold. "

- **Technical Experts**
- **Communicators**
- **Listeners**
- **Collaborators**

Designing large software solutions is a highly complex task requiring architects to not only be Technical Experts but also to be effective Communicators, Listeners, and perhaps most important Collaborators. Effective architects recognize that the delivery of a software solution doesn't begin and end with design.

It begins with an abstract idea that must first be heard, then understood, and finally

synthesized into an architecture through
communication and collaboration across the
organization. The architect must be able to
coordinate with each group of stakeholders
effectively based on their needs and goals.

Stakeholders include Developers, Marketing,
Business, Project management, Quality
assurance, Change management, Executive,
and Customers many of which all have
competing goals. The role of the architect is
to collaboratively work with all the groups
involved to agree on a design and facilitate
construction of the solution. If that sounds
daunting that's because it is.

What an Architect is Expected to be Skilled At?

By now you may be saying to yourself well
wait a minute that sure sounds a lot different
than what I'm doing now as a senior
developer. The software architect role is

extremely challenging because you'll need to master a number of skills not all of which are technical. These are often thought of as soft skills but I think for most of us these are really the hard skills.

Architect skill set is a fusion of

- Leadership
- Technical
- Management

The architect skill set is a fusion of Technical, Management, and Leadership skills, skills not always possessed and often times not even desired by many senior developers.

What is an architect expected to be skilled at?

Technical	Management	Leadership
• Developer • Designer • Modeling • Keeping up new technologies	• Project Management • Problem Solving • Negotiation • Facilitation	• Vision • Self Directed • Decisive • Motivational • Inspirational • Confident • Committed • Delegate • Positive • Creative

Communication & Collaboration

As an architect you'll be expected to master a number of technical skills like development, design, modeling, and keeping up with new technologies. This last one may not seem like a skill but it's crucial for architects to keep up to date with new technology. The speed at which technology moves requires us to dedicate a significant amount of time to learning new technologies and discovering how they can be applied to our business problems. Most of these technical skills you've probably already mastered as a senior developer. These are the skills that have enabled you to move into the role of the architect. You'll continue to hone and develop them as an architect but now you have to expand your skill set to include those hard skills I mentioned like Project Management, Problem Solving, Negotiation, Facilitation to name a few. These management skills will help you in your new role as a team lead for your projects. As an architect one of your duties will be to organize and manage teams. If you're already doing this today as a senior developer than you may have already mastered some of the skills necessary. Additional skills that you may be less experienced with are those of a good leader. As an architect the entire team, not just technical will look to you for answers and direction. A good leader is able to form and communicate a Vision. A good leader's also Self Directed, Decisive, Motivational, Inspirational, Confident, Committed, has the ability to Delegate, Positive, and Creative. These skills will all be based on a foundation of your ability to communicate and collaborate with your teams. These are the two most fundamental and important skills you must possess to be an effective architect. All of us have spent many years developing our technical jobs. We've spent long hours learning about technology and applying it to solve problems. However, most of us have spent little time focusing on management techniques or leadership skills. Some of these skills come naturally to a few of us but others will need to dedicate time to learning and honing these skills to become effective architects. For me personally I spend time reading books and listening to podcasts on leadership and team building. There are also formal classes on management and leadership that you can attend, however I find that I learn best by observing the managers in my organization that are real leaders. you'll find that while there are a lot of managers in your organization there are a small number of individuals that truly know what it is to be a leader. Watch how these people interact with others and how they communicate, most important how others respond to them. Being a leader is not getting people to begrudgingly do the work you need them to, it's about connecting with people on a level where your goals become theirs and they personally feel committed to the success of whatever it is you're trying to achieve. This isn't a book on leadership so I won't spend any more time discussing this topic except to say that management and leadership are as important to your role as an architect as the technical portion. I know this doesn't sound as interesting as the technical stuff but like I said the soft skills are really the hard skills for most of us and it's going to take some time and effort on your part to master them.

What an Architect is Expected to Know?

What is an architect expected to know?
- **Broad knowledge**
- **General list of knowledge areas**
- **Architect role is very different from senior developer**
- **New challenges and opportunities to grow**
- **Senior Developer deep knowledge specific technologies**
- **Architect broad general knowledge**

What is an architect expected to know? Given the broad set of skills I've just outlined I'm sure you've already concluded that what you'll be expected to know is also very broad. Now it's important to note that the skills and knowledge items I'm outlining here are just general lists that I want you to be aware of. These are by no means meant to be comprehensive and know that you won't be expected to be an expert in all these areas your first day on the job. However, it's important to understand that stepping into the architect role is very different from what you're doing today as a senior developer. For some the skills, knowledge, and duties I'm outlining are not as interesting as the ones you're doing today as a senior developer. For others like me the role offers new challenges and opportunities to grow. It's important to understand the expectations and requirements of the role to know if it's a good fit for you. As a senior developer you're expected to have a deep knowledge in a

14

specific set of technologies. You're most likely a specialist in a certain platform or language. As an architect your breath of knowledge will be greatly expanded but the depth will be significantly reduced in some areas.

Non-Technical
•Leadership Techniques
•Management Techniques
•Business Processes
•Business & Enterprise Domain
Technical
•Architectural Concepts
•Architectural Patterns
•Architectural Styles
•Design Patterns
•Software Engineering
•Software Design
•Programming
•Platform Knowledge

An architect's knowledge areas can be separated into two categories: Technical and Non-Technical. These knowledge areas are directly related to the skills and duties required of this role. As an architect you'll be expected to be knowledgeable in Leadership Techniques and Management Techniques. Both will be essential when you're functioning as a team lead on a project or enterprise initiative. You'll also be expected to have a deep understanding of your organization's Business Processes and its Business & Enterprise Domain. In order to design and implement solutions for your organization you'll need to understand the business much more deeply than you did as a senior developer. Remember that as an architect you're not only delivering technical solutions you're leading initiatives within your organization to apply technical solutions to business problems. These are not always dropped in your lap as projects. You'll be expected to identify problems and suggest solutions that either reduce cost or provide revenue to your organization. The business does not have the technical knowledge or expertise that you do to propose technical solutions to its challenges. Your business stakeholders will know where their challenges lie and in many cases will suggest solutions to these problems. Your job as an architect is to not only evaluate these suggestions but to provide alternatives that might better solve the problem. An enterprise relies on its architects not only for delivering solutions but for technology related guidance. Your technical knowledge will continue to be leveraged and you should be well versed in technical areas such as Architectural Concepts including Architectural Patterns and Architectural Styles, Design Patterns, Software Engineering, Software Design, Programming, and Platform Knowledge. If you're not familiar with Architectural Patterns or Design Patterns then this should be a starting point for your additional education. Your deep knowledge in software engineering, design, and programming will continue to be important to the success of your projects. As an architect you'll not spend as much time programming as you did as a senior developer. You will need to make an effort to keep your programming skills and knowledge up to date with continuing education or by coding as much as possible. Later in this book I'll make some suggestions on how to keep coding as an architect.

Types of Architects

What is an architect expected to do?
- Duties of architect vary with role
- Duties overlap
- Many Titles
  - Enterprise
  - Solution
  - Solutions
  - Application
  - Software
  - Infrastructure...
- Confusing!

The duties of the software architect vary greatly based on what type of architect you are. In practice you'll find that there's a tremendous amount of overlap and confusion regarding the types of architects and what they do. To further confuse the point there are a number of titles related to architects like Enterprise Architect, Solution Architect, Solutions Architect, Application Architect, Software Architect, and even Infrastructure Architect. Many of these are even used interchangeably which is also very confusing. For the purposes of this book I'm going to identify and define the three main types of software architects. I'm then going to focus on the two that this book is primarily concerned with.

Enterprise Architect
- Strategic Architect
- People
- Process
- Information Flow
- Business Processes

- Strategic Goals
- Business Strategies
- Technical Strategies
- Roadmaps
- Not all software
- Align with business

Solutions Architect

- Tactical Architect
- Cross Domain
- Cross-functional
- System Interactions
- Frameworks
- Infrastructure
- Interoperability
- Horizontal Problems
  - Roadmaps
  - Guidance
- Cross Cutting
  - Reuse
  - Process
  - Guidance
- Strategic Solutions

Application Architect

- Operational Architect
- Single Application(s)
- Single Technologies
  - Web
  - Desktop
  - Mobile
- Component Reuse
- Maintainability
- Detailed Designs
- Components
- Modules
- Classes
- Libraries

- Languages
- Reuse with business unit

The first type of architect is the Enterprise Architect. The Enterprise Architect is the Strategic Architect in your organization. He or she is primarily concerned with People, Process, and Information Flow within the organization. And how enterprise software systems support Business Process and Strategic Goals of the organization. This architect is also concerned with making sure that Business and Technical Strategies align. Enterprise Architects provide Roadmaps that guide the direction of information technology within the organization. Software based solutions are not the only concern of the Enterprise Architect. These architects are aligned more with business than with technology. The Solutions architect is the Tactical Architect. He or she is concerned with Cross Domain, Cross-Functional problems such as System Interactions, Frameworks, Infrastructure and Interoperability. This architect's focus is on Horizontal Problems providing Roadmaps and Guidance that can be shared across problem domains or even business units. And these architects are additionally concerned with horizontal Cross Cutting concerns like Reuse and technology related Process and Guidance. These architects are not necessarily assigned to a single business unit but may specialize in technology or verticals within the organization. They design and help implement solutions that support the strategic goals of the organization. The Application Architect is the Operational Architect. He or she is concerned with the Single Application or

Applications and technologies that support a business unit. They are focused on Component Reuse and Maintainability of these applications. This architect will create very detailed designs for solutions within his or her problem domain. They're not as concerned with systems interactions as with Components, Modules, Classes, Libraries, and Languages. These architects are technology and business specialists that focus on a suite of applications pertinent to their business unit. These architects also provide horizontal cross cutting solutions but they're typically targeted within the business unit. Because this book is primarily concerned with software solutions and not with process we'll not spend any time discussing the role of the enterprise architect as I just defined it. I realize that many of you probably hold the enterprise architect title but if you're reading this book and are primarily concerned with delivering software solutions and not process then you're either a Solutions Architect or an Applications Architect regardless of your title. This book will focus on the solutions and Application Architect roles in the enterprise. To further confuse the point no matter what your title is you'll probably perform the duties of both roles in your organization.

- **Perform duties of both Architects**
- **Solutions Architects rarely focus solely on tactical/strategic problems**
- **Solutions Architects deliver operational solutions**
- **Separate Teams for Architects**
    - **Solutions Architect Team**
    - **Applications Architect Team**

- May share the same title:
  Software Architect
- Two distinct roles:
  - Solutions Architect
  - Application Architect
  - No matter what your title you
    may perform the duties of both

It's been my experience that Solutions Architects are rarely allowed to focus solely on tactical or strategic problems. We're almost always assigned to operational level projects that deliver solutions to a group of users. In practice many organizations have separates teams for each type of architect. They have one team that contains a group of Solutions Architects and one or many teams of Applications Architects. Sometimes they'll even all share the same title of software architect; this can be very confusing. However the important point I'm trying to make here is that there are two distinct roles: Solutions Architect and Application Architect. And in many organizations no matter what your title you'll perform the duties I'm going to outline here of each role.

Non-Technical Duties: Project

What is an architect expected to do?
- Broad set of duties
- Solutions vs. Application Architect?
- Role Varies between organizations
- Core set of duties

Like skills and knowledge a Software Architect's duties are very broad and truly depend on whether you're acting as a

Solutions Architect or an Application's
Architect. The role will also vary greatly
between organizations, however there are a
core set of duties you'll encounter in most
organizations.

Non-Technical Duties –the hard skills

- Projects
- People
- Process

Let's begin with the duties that you're most
likely not that excited about. Yes, these are
the non-technical duties or as I said earlier
these are the hard skills for most of us.
Managing projects, People, and Process is an
extremely important part of the role of the
architect.

Non-Technical Duties –the hard skills

- Manage the Project
  - May have project manager
    assigned to your project
  - Good project managers are
    incredible assets
  - Good project managers are
    hard to find
  - Be prepared to take on the role
    of the project manager

One aspect of your job as an architect may
include managing a project from beginning
to end. In many organizations you'll have a
project manager assigned to your project to
help manage the team. When this is the case
you'll find that having a good project
manager on your team in an incredible asset
that will allow you to spend more time
focusing on the technical portions of the
project. However, it's been my experience
that good managers are really hard to find,
they're like white leopards you don't see

them very often but when you do it's an incredible experience. Over the book of my career I've worked with a few talented project mangers that understood how to manage a technical team and were truly invested in the success of the project. Hopefully your organization has a number of these talented individuals but if not you must be prepared to take on this role if needed.

Non-Technical Duties: People - Building a Team

Non-Technical Duties –the hard skills
- Build a Team
  - Required for every project
  - Not only developers on this team

The ability to build a team is a critical part of the software architect role also because it's something you'll be required to do for just about every project you work on. While you're most likely very comfortable working with a development team the teams that you'll work with as an architect will include many individuals that aren't all developers. Your team will include Project Managers, Quality Assurance Testers, Business Analysts, Change Management Administrators, Database Administrators, Network Engineers, and of course developers. Now this is only the technical side. As an architect your team will also include Subject Matter Experts from the business and other operational folks that will have a vested interest in the project.

Non-Technical Duties -People
- Even small projects take a team
- Facilitate collaboration between team members
- Architects lead the charge
  - Guidance
  - Technical Decision
- Project Managers can help
- Architects job is to organize:
  - Solution
  - Team
  - Deliverable Order
  - Break solutions into manageable pieces
- Sometimes you are the project manager
- Organizing & Managing team is critical to delivering project

Even the smallest projects seem to require an army to complete. While you're not interacting with all of these members on a daily basis you will be leading the effort which requires you to facilitate the collaboration between each of these team members. They will look to you as the person leading the charge, providing guidance and making technical decisions on the direction of the project. A good project manager can help with much of this but remember organizing the solution, the team, the and the deliverable order is typically up to the architect. The project manager will look to you to provide guidance on how to organize the project into manageable pieces that he or she can manage. On smaller teams it's sometimes up to the architect to manage the project without a project mangers involvement. Organizing and managing your team will be critical to delivering your project. I have found that separating your project into subsystems that can be worked on simultaneously is one of the most effective ways to organize your team. Break your solution up into pieces that can be worked on independently and then organize your team so that each subsystem has its own resources and schedule. I have found that using an iterative approach is the most effective way to manage a project. It provides incremental winds which help motivate and push forward your projects by setting achievable short term goals.

Non-Technical Duties -Project
- Collaborate with team
  - Foster ownership
  - Commitment
- Leading a team
  - Empower
  - Team sets goals
  - Team sets milestones
  - Architect works with team
- Checkout the Pluralsight courses on Agile

Collaborate with your team when planning each subsequent schedule and deliverables. Including them in planning will help foster ownership and commitment within your team. Leading a team isn't about dictating schedule and milestones it's about empowering your team to set its own goals and milestones and then working right alongside them to get the job done.

Non-Technical Duties: Process

Non-Technical Duties -Process
- **Even small projects take a team**
  - **Process is your best friend**
- **Clearly defined & repeatable process must be adopted**
- **Develop your own processes**
  - **Tailor to your organization and methodology**
  - **Create a set of repeatable procedures**

Delivering even a small software project takes a team and when working with a team process is your best friend. A clearly defined and repeatable process must be adopted if you're going to succeed. Keep this in mind as you're learning this new role. Keep a list of things that work and develop them into processes that you can perform on each and every project. Your processes will be specific to your organization and the methodology you're using but even within a defined methodology there are lots of room to customize. Developing your process into a set of repeatable procedures will save you time and frustration in the future.

Non-Technical Duties -Process
- **Personal set of documents to guide projects and duties**
  - **Simple bulleted lists**
  - **Continually update**
  - **Use any tool that allows you to create and organize lists**
  - **Working set of documents**
- **3 Goals**

- More effective through continual process evaluation and improvement
- Delegate process
- Teaching aid
- Share process documents with team

It may sound like overkill but personally I keep a working set of documents that guide my projects and duties. These are simple bulleted lists that I continually change as I discover practices that can help to make me more effective. Whenever I work on a process -- something that I know I'm going to perform a number of times I spend a little extra time developing a simple bulleted list of steps that I follow. These days I use Google Docs but you can do this with OneNote or any other tool that allows you to create and organize simple bulleted lists. These are a working set of documents that I will continually modify every time I repeat the process and discover something that can make it more efficient. The intention is threefold. First it helps me to become more effective because I continually evaluate and improve my processes. Second if I can follow these steps then so can someone else so once documented this process can be assigned to someone else to perform. Lastly these documents are great teaching aids because I can share them with my peers that are performing the same duties I am. This helps me with projects too because I often share these documents with the team to instruct them on the procedures that will follow. If you're skeptical then I would suggest you adopt this tactic for a few months with just a few processes, you'll discover the tremendous value for yourself.

Non-Technical Duties: Support

Non-Technical Duties -Support
- Support Management, Business and Organization
  - Technological Insights
- Business relies on your:
  - Expertise
  - Experience
  - Foresight
  - Introduce/Evaluate technical solutions
  - When NOT to apply technology

Support Management, Business and the Organization by providing insights into the ways technology can be leveraged to solve business problems. Often business leaders will not have the same insight you do into relevant technologies. They will rely on your Expertise, Experience, and Foresight to introduce or evaluate technical solutions. It will be equally important to the organization to identify where not to apply technology as a solution because of cost, complexity, or unnecessary risk. You will use your technical experience and knowledge to support your management team, business, and organization.

Non-Technical Duties: Leadership

Non-Technical Duties -Leadership
- Technical Leader
    - Technical Team
    - Business
    - Management
    - Organization
- You are a technical representative
    - Company, Division, Line of Business
    - Make a good impression
- Architects provide solutions to the business
    - Don't underestimate business creativity
    - Must be open and willing to understand problems
    - Quick to act

Being a Technical Leader is most likely something that comes natural to most people that have gravitated to this position. It's important to provide leadership not only to the Technical Team but also to the Business, Management, and Organization as a whole. Remember you're a technical representative for your company, division, or Line of Business. Often you're the only interface to the technical team that the business will interact with. The impression you leave them with is how they will regard the entire division, department, or team. They look to you to provide solutions and insights to their pain points, not to slow down or obstruct their goals. If you're unable or unwilling to

29

help solve their problems they may look outside your department or even the organization for solutions. Don't underestimate the creativity of the business to solve problems without your input. If you want to be part of the conversation you must be open and willing to understand their problems and quick to act in solving them. Over the years I've been in many conversations where the business has shared with me how some enterprising individual in their department has solved a business need with an access application or spreadsheet or even web application that they've now outgrown or no longer have support for because that person's moved on. If we want to be part of the discussion we need to be open and willing to solve problems when the business brings them to us.

Non-Technical Duties -Leadership

- Technical Leader
- Teaching & Mentoring
- Helps improve colleagues skills
- Helps project authority and expertise
- Build relationships
- Training benefits everyone

As a Technical Leader you should not only be teaching and mentoring junior developers but anyone that generally expresses interest in a subject within your area of influence or expertise. Training and mentoring is a great way to help your colleagues improve their skills. It also can help you to project authority or expertise in an area. Additionally these opportunities help you to build relationships within the teams that you'll be relying on to deliver solutions. Training and mentoring provides benefit not only to the people you're helping but to you as well.

Non-Technical Duties -Leadership

- Leading a Project
  - Create a Vision
  - Facilitate delivery of solution
  - Delegate
  - Never make yourself the critical path on development tasks
  - Your job is to support and enable the entire team
  - Give junior team members the opportunity to learn & contribute
  - Don't spread yourself too thin on development tasks

We've already touched on this a bit but Leading a Project is something that you'll do quite often as an architect. Being a Technical Leader requires you to create a vision and solution that can be explained and adopted by the team. Providing the leadership necessary to the team that helps facilitate the delivery of the solution is one of the primary duties that you'll perform. I use the term projects here in the generalist of terms but please not that projects not only encompass a line of business applications but also strategic and tactical initiatives for your organization. These initiatives may or may not result in software being produced. They could be implementing out of box solutions or even just be process related. Before I move on to the technical duties I want to bring up an important point. Many of us mistakenly believe that it's sometimes faster to do things ourselves than to spend the time teaching and delegating tasks. This is something I did early on and paid the price more than a few times. While it's okay to assign development tasks to yourself it's never a good idea to make yourself the critical path on any task. Your ability to support the entire team will be critical to the success of your projects. If you're in the weeds working on a task that any number of developers could accomplish then this is not helping the project. While it's often true that our junior members of the team don't work as quickly as you might it's important to give them the opportunity to learn and contribute so that they can grow into more senior developers. It's also important that you don't spread yourself too thin on development tasks that could be assigned to any number of developers on your team. They may do the job a little differently or even slower but it will get done and your time is better spent facilitating not performing the individual tasks.

Technical Duties: Creating The Architecture

Technical Duties
- Create an architecture
- Small part of the job
- Architecting a solution
  - 3 primary steps

Let's move on now to the Technical Duties where most of us feel a lot more comfortable. Technical duties are the ones that you'll most likely have excelled in as a senior engineer before you made the decision to become an architect. Creating an architecture that provides a solution to a business problem is something you have most likely performed many times in your career today. You may have already noted that this is but a small part of the job you'll be performing for your organization as an architect. We will delve into this much more deeply in the next module but architecting a solution involves 3 primary steps.

Select the Architecture
- Style
  - Client Server
  - Message Bus
  - Service Oriented Architecture
  - Domain Driven Design
  - Layered Architecture
  - Component Based
  - ...
- Pattern
  - MVC
  - Publish/Subscribe
  - Request/reply
  - Peer-to-peer
  - ...

The first is selecting which architectural style or styles to apply and which architectural patterns to leverage. In some cases your solution may not even include constructing a product at all. It may be better for your organization to purchase an off the shelf product or redeploy an existing product to solve a business need. It is your job to make the recommendations that will allow your organization to weigh these alternatives and decide which direction to proceed.

Technical Duties
- Design a solution that solves business problem
- Not just drawing rectangles on a white board
- Solving a multifaceted problem

The second step is to design a solution that solves a particular problem for your organization. Designing a solution is not just about drawing bunch of rectangles on a white board it's about solving a multifaceted problem. The architect's challenge is to design a solution that is both technically and organizationally feasible. That is to say you're designing a solution that takes into account many factors that are specific to your particular organization. These may include Resourcing, Cost, Project Duration, the Teams Experience, Deployed Infrastructure, Business Processes, Technical Team Processes, and even Methodologies.

Design the Architecture
- Understand organizational tolerances
  - Business
  - Technical
- Design solutions
  - Solve problem
  - Can be delivered

It's your job to fully understand the organizational tolerances both Business and Technical before drawing your first rectangle on the white board. Your job is to design solutions that not only solve the problem but can be delivered. After all if your solution is never implemented then no matter how good your design it's failed.

Document the Architecture

- Design and Documentation solve two distinct problems
- Design –Solve the problem
  - Understanding entire problem
  - Creating technical solution
- Documentation –Communicating the solution
  - Technical & Non-Technical Stakeholders
  - Expression of the design
- Format and Style are not important
- Understanding across the organization is paramount
- Goal: Effectively communicate solution
- Doesn't have to be UML
- Standards are important

The third step is documenting the architecture. I've separated design and documentation here because each solve different problems. Designing is the process of solving the problem. It is understanding the entire problem and creating a technical solution that meets the needs of the business and most importantly solves the business problem. Documenting is how we communicate the solution to others both Technical and Non-technical. It's the expression of the design in terms that can be understood and acted on to construct the solution. The terminology and diagram types are not as important as how well they're understood in your organization. It doesn't matter if you use UML or a bunch of rectangles the goal was to effectively communicate the solution not conforming to a standard that has not been adopted or not even fully understood by your organization.

If there's not a standard in place related to architecture documentation then it's your job to put one in place. In the next module we'll review some sample architectural diagrams that you may use as a starting point but finding the right standard will be an important part of defining your processes and most importantly communicating your solutions to the team.

Technical Duties: The Rest of Your Duties

Evaluate Architecture
- Evaluate your own architecture
- Evaluate peers architecture
- Evaluating existing architecture
- Evaluation
  - Objective
  - How well solution solves the problem
  - Don't be overcritical or unconstructive
  - Addresses quality attributes
  - Meets goals and project and organization

Evaluating your own architecture, evaluating other team member's architectures, and evaluating existing architectures is yet another duty you'll need to perform and become accustomed to. It's quite common for an architect to be on a team of architects. This could be an enterprised team of architects or an application architect that is embedded on a development team. In either case you'll be asked to evaluate your peers proposed architectures as well as architectures of existing solutions. It is important to understand that there are many solutions to any given problem. Your evaluation should be objective and not relative to how you would have solved the problem. Your evaluation should be with respect to how well the solution solves the problem relative to the goals and business needs of the organization. If you provide overly critical and unconstructive criticism then you may find yourself isolated from the team. I'm not saying you shouldn't be critical of others designs, you should be when a design does not solve the business problem adequately or does not address a quality attribute of the project. My point here is to evaluate the solution based on how well it meets the goals of the project and the organization.

Provide Technical Vision, Guidance & Leadership

- Technology related vision
- Technology related guidance
- Technology related leadership
- Guidance & Leadership when considering solutions
  - Custom application
  - Purchased products

I touched on vision, guidance, and leadership in the non-technical duties section so I won't go into too much detail here. As a technical duty I'm referring to vision, guidance, and leadership specifically related to technology and its use in projects and the organization as a whole. Your organization will look to you and your team for guidance and leadership when considering technological solutions. Some will be custom applications that you and your team build and others will be purchased products. As an architect your job is to provide guidance and leadership in these areas.

Evaluate technologies

- Apply technology to business problems
- Keep up with new technology
- Understand existing technology
- Guidance and Leadership –new & existing technology

Part of the architect's job is to evaluate technologies to understand how they can be applied to business problems. It's critical that you keep up with new technologies and how they can help to solve problems in your organization. You should also have a firm grasp of existing technologies and how they're utilized within your organization. Providing guidance and leadership with regard to new and existing technologies you get another area your organization will look to you for guidance.

Select Tools and Technology

- Tools & Technology
  - Development
  - Project & Processes

Selecting the tools and technology is another duty of the architect. You will be responsible for making sure the right tools and technologies are utilized. And these are not only the tools and technologies related to developing solutions but the tools and technologies your organization will utilize to support Projects and Processes within your organization.

Code

- Code if you are lucky
- Many non-coding duties
- Up to you how much coding you do
- Very difficult to both lead the team and code
- You assign logical groupings to team
- Can assign pieces to yourself
- Do not make yourself the critical path on any development task
- Your primary duty: Facilitate & Enable team
- Many architects don't code
- Extremely important for Architects to continue coding
- Benefits
    - Understanding new technologies
    - Keeping our existing skills sharp
    - Keep up with new technologies
    - Foster kinship with development team
- How?
    - Training Sessions
    - Prototyping

Code, if you're lucky -- yeah I said it -- if you're lucky you will still get to code. This is one of the most difficult things to come to terms with for most developers that become architects. Much of our time is spent doing non-coding activities, however in most cases it will be up to you how much coding you do. On small teams and projects you may find yourself coding right alongside the development team. On larger projects it's often very difficult to both lead a team and to code. One of the benefits of being the architect on the project is that you decide how the solution is separated into logical grouping and assigned to the team. In most cases you'll also have the ability to assign pieces of the project to yourself if desired. I mentioned this before and I'm going to mention it again here, I recommend that you do not make yourself the critical path on any part of the solution. Your primary duty is to Facilitate and Enable the team to deliver the project not to code it yourself. Assign yourself tasks that don't hold up progress if you're pulled in other directions. Now while many archit4ects do not code I feel it's extremely important that we continue coding as much as possible. Coding provides a number of benefits including understanding new technologies and keeping our existing skills sharp. Architects that don't code often lose some of the skills that put them in the role in the first place which could impact our ability to design solutions and even estimate work effort. Technology never stands still so it's important not only to keep up but to experiment with new technologies, this helps us to understand and level set expectations you'll have of your development teams. It also helps to foster a kinship between you and the development team. One technique that I've used successfully over the years is to conduct training sessions for development teams. Creating a sample application and preparing for a presentation in front of a group of people tends to focus your learning. Not to mention that teaching is one of the best ways to learn something. Your development teams are an extremely forgiving audience and truly appreciative of any effort to help keep them up with technology. Sharing your sample applications and knowledge through teaching is a great way to keep coding. Prototyping is yet another way to keep your fingers in the coding pie. I often create prototypes to demonstrate technologies or portions of solutions that are new or unfamiliar to the team. This is a great way for you to continue coding, to teach and to provide valuable samples of new and unfamiliar technologies.

Technical Duties: What Not to Do

What an architect should not do
- Ivory Tower Architect
    - Casts down designs from on high
    - Ineffective Technique
    - Makes us all look bad
    - Do not become this type of Architect
- Team effort
- Must be done collaboratively
- Team will provide:
    - Feedback
    - Insight
- Effective Leaders:
    - Work alongside team
    - Listen to feedback
    - Guide Team
    - React to challenges

I want to take a moment to discuss what an architect should not do. I want to mention the Ivory Tower Architect. We've all worked with at least one of them over the years. This is the person that casts down his or her designs from on high to be implemented by their subjects on the development team. I'm sure I don't need to tell you how ineffective this technique is, not to mention what it does for how people view those of us with a title of architect. Take care not to become this type of architect. Creating complex software solutions is a team effort and must be done collaboratively with your entire team. They'll offer valuable feedback and insights to the solution. Always remember that an effective leader doesn't lead a team by giving them the game plan and just going home. They're right there alongside their players listening to feedback, guiding the team, and reacting to challenges that the team encounters.

Why Do We Need Architects?

Why do we need Software Architects?
- The need for an architect increases with the complexity
- The more complex a solution the more likely it could fail
- Long drawn out failures more common
- Most common reasons projects fail:
    - Project does not achieve business goals
    - Project takes too long
    - Project costs too much
- Experienced architects mitigate risk
- Experienced architects bring:
    - Vision
    - Leadership

- Structure
- Experience
- Success can only be planned
  - Strong Leader
  - Unified vision
  - Careful planning
  - Structure
  - Process

Is it possible to create software applications without an architect? Absolutely. After all software developers write the software, not the architect. However as software systems become more and more complex the need for an architect becomes more and more important. The more complex a software application is the more likely it is that the project could fail. In most cases this is not a complete failure where the product isn't delivered, it's more common to see a long drawn out failure where the project either takes more time than was originally planned or costs twice as much than was anticipated. These sorts of failures are more subtle but one could argue more damaging because the organization continues to sink money and resources into projects that even once delivered may not meet the business goals that originally drove it. In the case where projects take too long business opportunities that once drove the project may have disappeared. It's been my experience that the most common reasons projects fail are the project doesn't achieve business goals, it takes too long, or it costs too much. Having an experienced architect on the project is no silver bullet but it does mitigate some of the risks associated with complex software projects. He or she brings Vision,

Leadership, Structure, and Experience to the team. Success can only be planned; it can't be left to chance by expecting a group of technologists to self organize, identify a single vision, and march forward to completion. It requires a Strong leader, a Unified Vision, Careful planning, Structure, and Process. Next I'll address each of the most common failures I just listed and discuss how an experienced architect could help overcome these challenges.

Why Do We Need Architects: Meeting Business Goals

Meeting Business Goals
- Identify how a solution will achieve its business goals
    - Project scope and functional requirements
    - Business stakeholders
- High level architecture presentation
    - Express the design on paper
    - Explains interpretation of the business goals
    - Collaborative
- Goals:
    - Synthesizes all the formal and informal inputs
    - Expresses in a design
    - Communicates
    - Feedback
    - Understand business goals
- Collaboration
    - Listen

- Speak
- Guide business toward solution

One of the primary directives of the architect is to clearly identify how a solution will achieve its business goals. Business goals are identified formally on the project scope and functional requirements documents and informally through discussions with business stakeholders. The architect incorporates all these inputs and expresses them into a high level architecture that he or she presents back to the business for feedback. This process is important because it accomplishes two goals. First it forces the architect to think through the solution and express the design on paper. These documentation artifacts will be used downstream in the project for many purposes but this is the first step and a critical one. Second this presentation is important because this is where the architect explains his or her interpretation of the business goals. And this meeting is collaborative it should not be a lecture. The archit4ect will receive many questions and lots of feedback. He or she will know if they're on target and if there are parts of the solution that need more attention. I'll spend more time on this topic later in the book but the important point here is that the architect forms two functions at the inception of the project. He or she synthesizes all the formal and informal inputs provided by the business stakeholders, expresses them in a design intended for this particular audience and then communicates it with the intention of receiving feedback from the team. From the inception of the project we can determine if we understand the business goals of the project before a single line of code is written. This in itself does not guarantee success but it's much more appealing than beginning with code. This is not the only time this type of collaboration should occur between an architect and the business stakeholders but it sets the stage and tone for the entire project. And this is how the architect creates a feedback loop between themselves and the business. Collaboration is the key to the success of any project. An architect must listen as much as speak this team. He or she will set expectations, identify non-functional requirements, and most importantly guide the business towards a solution that provides the greatest return given the time and budgetary constraints of the project.

Why Do We Need Architects: Project Duration

Project Duration
- Many dangers when a project takes too long to complete
    - Business opportunity may disappear
    - Organization may lose interest
    - Other projects may be impacted
    - ...
- Architect helps mitigate this risk
- Divide project into subsystems
    - Each worked independently
    - Abstract complexity
    - Smaller workable chunks

- Small teams working concurrently
- Benefits:
  - More efficient
  - Small wins motivate
  - Hit dates more accurately
- Realistic time and resourcing estimates
- Components are more easily estimated
  - Top down estimates
  - Bottom up estimates
  - Set realistic expectations with business
- Determine project feasibility based on top down estimates
- Predict project duration based on bottom up estimates

There are many dangers that occur when a project takes too long to complete. The business opportunity may disappear, the organization may lose interest, other projects may be impacted because resources are not available, the list goes on. An architect's presence on a project can help mitigate this type of risk. A common architectural practice when designing complex systems is to subdivide them into subsystems, grouped by responsibility. Each of these subsystems can then be worked on independently by the team. The logical view of the system is intended to simplify the whole by grouping complex processes into black boxes abstracting away the complexity of each subsystem. After all the entire team doesn't need to understand or even be concerned with the complexities of every subsystem they just need to understand their responsibilities and the interfaces to others. Dividing large projects into smaller workable chunks also helps a team work more efficiently. This practice naturally lends itself to running smaller teams concurrently. Each team can work independently toward their goal of completing a subsystem. Working this way not only helps with efficiency but with motivation. Teams feel a sense of completion when their assignments are completed and they're more energized to conquer the next task. Separating large complex projects into smaller more efficient chunks that can be worked on independently and concurrently often helps drive these projects toward hitting their target dates more accurately. Realistic time and resourcing estimates are also extremely important to accurately plan the duration of a project. By dividing the system up into its component pieces it's more easily estimated. Initially broad based top down estimates are provided by the architect but its teams are assigned and detailed designs completed, development teams can provide more accurate estimates based on experience with specific tools and technologies being utilized. These bottom up estimates are often more accurate as more detail is known about the system. It is the job of the architect to make sure that this portion of the process occurs and that realistic expectations are set with the business stakeholders. This isn't to say that the architect's estimates are not accurate but they're often created in inception of the project where many details are opaque. These top down estimates are important because they allow the business to decide whether or not the project is feasible. However the bottom up estimates from the development will always be a more accurate reflection of the actual duration of a project. The architect's role is an important part of the process and provides much value in mitigating the risk of project time overruns.

Why Do We Need Architects: Project Cost

Project Cost
- Architects have much influence on cost
- Architects quantify costs of components
    - Understand which are more complex & risk prone
    - Guide business to less costly & less complex solution
- Business can't quantify cost
    - Need vs. Want
- Architect helps business understand needs with regard to cost
- Architect should help understand cost associated with project
    - Provide alternatives
    - Same goal
    - Lower costs
    - Reduced complexity
- Focus on what they are trying to accomplish?
- Always ask why
    - Listen
    - Understand

- Needs and wants are often combined
  - Asserted as facts
- Whole process is a negotiation
- Job of the Architect:
  - Listen
  - Identify needs
  - Guide
- Not easy but necessary to keep projects within budget

Architects are of tremendous value at the inception of a project because they can help guide business stakeholders through technical quagmires that may become very costly to implement. Rarely does a business enter into a project without regard for return on investment. As an architect we have the experience and knowledge to quantify the cost of each component part of a solution. We know what components are more complex or risk prone and can guide our business stakeholders to solutions that meet their goals while reducing the complexity of a solution as much as possible. Business stakeholders only have in mind what they want to accomplish but they have no way to quantify the cost. They just know that they need a system to do x, y, and z but they have no idea the cost of each part. X and y may be needs and z is a want but not required to meet the business goal. The architect's job is to help business stakeholders understand their needs with regard to cost. Many times I've entered into discussions with business stakeholders describing what they believe the solution should be and once I quantify the cost of each component they often identify the components that are truly required for success. These stakeholders understand the importance of cost when making business decisions but with no background in software development they often let the scope of the project grow without regard. The job of the architect is not to tell the business stakeholder what is needed but to help them understand the cost associated with their project and to provide alternatives that might achieve the same goal at lower cost and reduced complexity. The focus should always be on what they are trying to accomplish. We should always ask why when presented with project requirements. We need to listen to responses so that we truly understand the goals and needs of the business. Often when entering into these discussions needs and wants will be combined and asserted as facts but make no mistake this whole process is a negotiation. The job of the architect is to Listen, Identify needs, and Guide your audience to the best solution with regard to constraints both technical and financial. This is not an easy task but necessary to help keep projects within budget.

Why Do We Need Architects: Righting the Ship

Righting the Ship
- Architects help right the ship
- Many reasons why project veer off course
  - Too long to complete
  - Cost more than anticipated

- Reduce time and cost
  - Reduce scope
  - Identify complex components
  - Eliminate or move complex components
  - Effective resource management
- More developers doesn't always help
  - As developers increase so does management and ramp up time
  - Architect can help identify where most effective to add resources

When projects begin to veer off course an architect can help right the ship. There are any number of reasons that a project can veer off course. Taking longer to complete or costing more than originally anticipated are just a few examples. One method for reducing the time and cost is reducing scope. The architect can help the business stakeholders identify the more complex and time consuming pieces a project that might be eliminated or moved to other phases of the project. He or she is also able to help with resource management. Bringing more developers onto a project does not always help as much as the business might expect. We as architects understand that as the number of developers increase so does the time needed to ramp up and manage the team but our business probably doesn't understand it the same way we do. An architect can help the project team identify where it would be most effective to add resources.

Why do we need Software Architects?

- Software architects are a valuable asset to organization
- Provided tangible examples:
    - Project Duration
    - Project Cost
    - Business Goals

I realize that most everyone reading this book most likely already believes that software architects are a valuable asset to the organization however I wanted to spend a little time providing some tangible examples that discuss how an architect could directly benefit a project with regard to Duration, Cost, and Business Goals.

Summary

Summary
- Software Architect role is very different from that of a senior developer
- Being skilled technically is only 1/3rdof the equation
- Who is a software architect
- What a software architect is expected to be skilled at
- What a software architect is expected to know
- What a software architect is expected to do in the organization
- Why organizations need software architects
- How a software architect might help a project that has veered off course

It should be pretty apparent to you by now that being a software architect is much different from being a senior developer. While being skilled technically is very important it's only a third of the equation. Some of you may even be reconsidering your decision to become an architect at this point. Well let me reassure you that while everything I just listed is part of the job you won't be expected to be an expert at everything on your first day. As a matter of fact even those of us that have occupied the job for many years are still learning and working on the skills I just listed. So hang in there, it's going to be a bumpy ride. In this module we covered who is a software architect, what an architect is expected to be skilled at, what an architect is expected to know, and what an architect is expected to do in the organization. In the last portion of the module we covered why organizations need software architects and discussed a few examples of how an architect might help a project that's veered off course.

The Software Architect's Role in the Project Life Cycle

Introduction

The architect's role in the project life cycle
- Project Phases
  - Project Initiation
  - Assembling the team

- Requirements
- Design
- Construction
- Testing
- Implementation

This is the module, The Architect's Role in the project life cycle. In this module we're going to review all the phases of a typical project and outline the architect's role in each. We'll discuss in detail what an effective architect should be doing in each phase of the project. We're going to cover Project Initiation, Assembling the team, Requirements, Design, Construction, Testing, and Implementation. Now this is meant to be a general list of Project Phases that occur no matter what methodology your organization is using. I'm not suggesting this is a hard and fast list of things that every architect does on every project in every organization, this is meant to be a representation of the things that many architects do as part of their role when leading a team to deliver a project. My intention is to help you to understand the responsibilities of the architect in the enterprise when leading a project. Many people mistakenly believe that architects are only involved in the design phase of the project; however, this just isn't the case. Effective architects participate from beginning to end and play an important role in the success of the project. Now let's get started.

Project Initiation

The architect's role in the project life cycle
- **Project Initiation**
  - **Projects are initiated by LOB**
    - **New product**
    - **Enhancement to existing product**
  - **Projects assigned to architect most experienced in:**
    - **Technology**
    - **Business domain**
  - **Multiple architects may be assigned**
  - **Outline a viable solution**
  - **Get comfortable with ambiguity**
  - **Listen to your stakeholders**
    - **Understand business goals**
  - **Identify the most complex pieces of the solution**
    - **Interop points of solution**
    - **Most rigid & time consuming**
  - **Identify portions of the solution that will most greatly impact:**
    - **Timeline**
    - **Cost**
  - **Architecturally significant portions of the project**
  - **Consultant providing recommendations**

Project Initiation is the first phase in the project life cycle. Projects are typically initiated by a line of business that has identified a new product or enhancement to an existing product. Projects are typically assigned to the architect most experienced with the particular Technology or Business domain. If the product spans multiple technologies or business units then multiple architects may be assigned. The first goal of these architects during project initiation is to outline a viable solution across technologies or lines of business. At this point in the project, requirements are very vague so get comfortable with ambiguity. Much time is spent listening to your stakeholders trying to understand the business goals of the project. It's imperative during this phase of the project to identify the most complex pieces of the solution. These are most often found where your solution will be required to interoperate with systems outside your realm of influence or control. These dependencies are typically the most rigid and time consuming to construct. It's the job of the architect to identify the portions of the solution that will most greatly impact the Timeline and Cost of the project. These are often referred to as the architecturally significant portions of the project. During Project Initiation, the architect's role is to act as a Consultant, providing recommendations related to technologies or approach.

Project Initiation
- Sizing the project
  - High level cost and resource estimates

- Decide project viability
- Project Sizing
  - General Connotation
  - Doesn't imply commitment
  - General expectation to work effort
- Sometimes project end here
- High Level Estimates
  - Feasibility decision
  - Based on what you know today
  - Revisited later
- Project Sizing
  - Effective Tool
  - Easy to understand
  - Separate into S,M,L buckets
  - Buckets identify resources and duration
- Examples
  - Small: <5 people / < 6 months
  - Medium: 5-10 people / 3 to 12 months
  - Large: 25+ / 6 -12+ months
- Sizing project helps business determine:
  - Number of resources
  - Project duration
  - Provide enough value
- Project requirements too vague to provide accurate estimates
- Sizing includes all resources

- Sizing helps business to determine project viability

Sizing the project properly is the next step during Project Initiation. The architect often provides high level cost and resource estimates that can be used by the business to decide whether or not the solution is viable. I hesitate to even call these estimates as they might be interpreted as firm commitments to business stakeholders. A better term for what we're doing is Project Sizing. It has more of a General Connotation and doesn't imply commitment, but a general expectation as to work effort. In many cases, a project won't progress past this point. These estimates are only being used to make Feasibility decisions. Remember they're based on what you know today and will be revisited later when we have a clearer understanding of the project requirements. Project Sizing is an effective tool because it's very easy to understand for all stakeholders involved. In its simplest form, projects can be separated into Small, Medium, and Large buckets, where each bucket identifies numbers of resources and duration. Examples would be a Small project where 5 or fewer people are on a team and it takes less than 6 months to complete; Medium, where you have 5-10 people on a team and it takes 3-12 months to complete; or Large where you have 25 or more people on a team and it takes 6-12+ months to complete. Sizing a project allows the business stakeholder to determine whether or not the project can be resourced properly, delivered within time constraints, and if it provides enough value given resource and costs. Projects are often too vague at this point to provide detailed and accurate hour estimates. Additionally, when hour estimates are provided, they often only account for construction which doesn't adequately account for the total resource needs of the project. Sizing the project properly to include all resources needed is extremely important at this phase and will help the business to determine if the project will proceed to the next phase.

Project Initiation

- Know your stakeholders
    - Who are your stakeholders?
        - organization leaders
        - enterprise architects
        - project managers
        - business users
    - Understand their needs and goals
        - Identify preferred solutions
        - Business goals
        - Quality attributes
    - Understand the business domain
        - Interview users
        - Build relationships

Knowing who your stakeholders are is yet another aspect of Project Initiation. Important stakeholders at this point are organization leaders, enterprise architects, project managers, and business users. Time must be dedicated to understanding their needs, goals, and desires. Interview these stakeholders to get familiar with their preferred solutions, business goals, and quality attributes. If you're not familiar with the business domain, this is also when the architect must invest some time understanding the line of business. Reach out to potential users of the system and interview them about their role as it relates to the project. Effective architects build relationships during Project Initiation that will be invaluable resources as the project gets underway.

Project Initiation

- Know what questions to ask
    - Create a general list for your interview
    - Let the responses drive the interview
    - Listen intently
    - Repeat & rephrase questions
    - Make sure you are clear on answers from all perspectives
    - Ask why a lot
        - Challenge the interviewee
        - Helps you understand problem
        - Helps interviewee understand if process adds value
    - Architect must understand problem entirely
        - Especially angles that seem unimportant

Knowing the right questions to ask at Project Initiation is extremely important. This is often accomplished by starting with a general list of questions, but then letting the responses drive you to what is really important. For this to be effective, you must intently listen to the responses, seeking to identify the hidden need that the stakeholders may not even realize they understand. Questions must be repeated and rephrased until you're clear on the answers from all perspectives. Ask why a lot, challenge the person you're interviewing to explain the reasoning behind why they're doing something. This will help you to understand the process, but may also help the interviewee to understand whether or not a task or process truly adds value. Architects solve difficult problems from many different angles. To be a truly effective architect you must understand them all, especially the angles that seem unimportant. When we don't have a complete understanding of them all, they often come back to bite us.

Project Initiation

- Developing and maintain strong feedback loops
  - Make business contacts
  - Get to know your stakeholders
  - Develop and maintain feedback loops
  - These stakeholders are your customers
  - They will support the adoption of your solution
  - This is the first step in building these important relationships

Developing and maintaining strong feedback loops is another essential part of the Initiation Phase of the project. At this point in the project, you're making contacts and getting to know business stakeholders. It's extremely important to develop and maintain strong feedback loops with these stakeholders as they are your customers. We'll discuss the importance of social networking shortly, but make no mistake these are people that will influence the users of your solution; you need their support and commitment to encourage the adoption of the solution. Soliciting feedback from these stakeholders is a first step in not only designing a solution that meets their needs, but in building these relationships.

Project Initiation
- Vision
  - Technical vision document
    - Overall vision for the solution
    - Core requirements
    - Key features
    - Quality attributes, constraints, goals
    - Evolves
    - Used as the basis for detailed designs
  - Singular concise vision
  - Vision drives all technical efforts moving forward

At this time, the architect is beginning to create a technical vision document that describes the overall vision or plan for the solution. This document outlines the core requirements from a very high level and is based on the key features identified by the business stakeholders. It should include any quality attributes, constraints or goals identified during the initial stakeholder interview. This document will evolve with the team's understanding of the requirements and will be used as the basis for more detailed designs that occur downstream. While the document is an important artifact, what is more important is that the team has a singular and concise vision of the solution.

This vision will drive all technical efforts moving forward.

Assembling the Team

The architect's role in the project life cycle
- Assemble the Team
  - Assemble your team of experts
  - Solutions are rarely designed by a single person
  - Architects rely on large social networks
  - Comprised of:
    - Architects
    - Senior Developers
    - Business Domain Experts
  - Lobby heavily for his core team to be assigned to project
  - Dual Purposes
    - Create a feedback loop of trusted domain and technology experts

The next phase of the project is not one formally identified in most software development methodologies, but make no mistake - this informal phase happens in every organization. Once the business agrees to proceed with the project, the architect will begin assembling a team of experts that will help design the solution. Designing a solution will often be assigned to a single architect; however, solutions are rarely designed by a single person without input from trusted and respected colleagues. Architects quite often rely on a large social network of experts in technology and business. This group of people may change depending on the business or platform domain, but it's typically comprised of other Architects, Senior Developers, and Business Domain Experts. This process is often informal, but the architect will lobby heavily to have his core team formally assigned to the project when it gets started. The assembly of the team has dual purposes. The first is to create a feedback loop of trusted domain and technology experts. The second is more subtle, but equally important to the success of the project.

Assemble the Team
- Garner Support
  - Collaboration builds:
    - Acceptance
    - Support
  - Foster a sense of ownership within core team
  - No place for egos
  - Architects ability to build a team contributes to projects success

Since the architect is not always part of the development team or business unit utilizing the solution, it's important for him to Garner Support from both teams. Collaborating with a team made up of representatives from both sides builds acceptance and support on both fronts. One of the goals of the architect is to foster a sense of ownership with a solution within the core team. This is a byproduct of the collaborative effort within the team. This is no place for egos or ivory tower mentalities. The architect's ability to

build a collaborative team will directly
contribute to the success of this project.
Assemble the Team

- Lobbying the technical team
    - Poll managers for resource
      availability
    - Success is determined by team
    - Lobbies for preferred
      developers
    - Longstanding relationships
      with development managers
    - Key to success is the right
      team
    - Architect builds core team
    - Architects lobby for best
      developers
    - Lobby both managers and
      developers

As a part of the assembly process, the
architect will reach out to technical
managers, polling them as to resource
availability. The architect knows that the
success of the project is determined by the
developers assigned, so he or she informally
lobbies development managers for preferred
developers. This informal negotiation
process is based on longstanding
relationships the architect has with
development managers and the development
team. This isn't to say that the architect is
unwilling to have junior members on his or
her team, but he knows the key to success is
having the right team. The architect is
building a core team of developers that will
be the foundation of the project. Architects
know which developers work best with his or
her leadership style and will lobby hard to
have these people assigned. The architect will

additionally contact developers directly to encourage them to request assignment to the team.

Assemble the Team
- Collaboration
  - Team is assembled with collaboration in mind
  - Core team is more committed when included in design process
  - Collaboration fosters commitment
  - Relationships formed here are invaluable

The architect assembles his team with collaboration in mind. This core team, both business and technical, will be more committed to the success and adoption of the architecture if they're included in the design process, much more so than if it was completed without their input. The relationships that are being formed are invaluable and will be leveraged both during and after completion of the project.

Requirements Definition

The architect's role in the project life cycle
- Requirements Definition
  - Functional requirements
    - Supportive
  - Non-functional requirements
    - Active

Requirements Definition is the next formal phase of the project. Requirements can be broken into two categories: Functional requirements and Non-Functional requirements. The architect plays a supportive role with regard to identifying Functional requirements, but a more active role in identifying Non-Functional requirements.

Requirements Definition
- Identify Requirements
    - Analysts don't always capture non-functional requirements
    - Functional requirements - What the system shall do
    - Non-functional requirements - What the system shall be

Most organizations have a group of analysts responsible for identifying and documenting Functional Requirements of the system; however, in my experience it's rare that they also capture Non-Functional Requirements. Business analysts are trained to identify behaviors and functions needed to support the business. They spend much of their time interviewing users to ferret out what the system should do. These requirements will used by the development team to understand specifically what the system shall do to be useful. In contrast, Non-Functional Requirements define constraints of the system or what a system shall be.

Requirements Definition
- Non-Functional Requirements
    - Non-functional requirements can greatly impact the architecture
    - Cross cutting concerns
    - Quality attributes
    - Architect actively identifies non-functional requirements

- Non-functional requirements guide decisions
  - Require tough decisions where goals conflict
- Important to capture non-functional requirements
  - Explain decisions about architecture

Non-Functional Requirements are important to the architect because they often greatly impact the architecture. They're the cross cutting concerns of the architecture, sometimes referred to as Quality attributes of the system. During the requirements phase of the project, the architect will actively identify Non-Functional Requirements. These attributes will guide the architects decisions during design, often requiring tough decisions where the attribute's goals conflict with each other. It's important to capture these requirements as they'll explain decisions made during design and after when others look at your architecture.

Requirements Definition
- Non-Functional Requirements
  - Examples are:
    - Accessibility
    - Availability
    - Configurability
    - Extensibility
    - Performance
    - Maintainability
    - Scalability
    - Security
    - Supportability
    - Testability
    - Usability

Some examples of the most common Non-Functional Requirements are Accessibility, Availability, Configurability, Extensibility, Performance, Maintainability, Scalability, Security, Supportability, Testability, and Usability.

Requirements Definition

- Non-Functional Requirements
  - Important for architect to understand functional requirements
    - May be incomplete for design
  - Architect identifies non-functional requirements
  - Architect interviews stakeholders
  - Identify as many as possible as early as possible
    - Helps insure design meets goals
  - Discuss business goals with stakeholders
    - Deduce non-functional requirements from business goals
  - Ask pointed questions
    - Use quality attributes list
    - Include cost and time explanations
  - Don't just ask if stakeholder wants a quality attribute like scalability
  - Ask questions like:
    - How many users are expected to use the system initially?

- What will this grow to in the future?
- What will the business impact be if the system is unavailable?
- Deduce need for scalability from answers to these questions
  - Weigh against infrastructure and development costs
- Results is non-functional scalability requirement and why

It's important for the architect to understand the functional requirements of the system; however, it's very unlikely that a complete set of requirements will be provided before system design begins. Because it's imperative that the software architect identify and understand the Non-Functional Requirements of the system before design begins, the architect must interview stakeholders to identify Non-Functional Requirements. The architect's goal is to identify as many as possible as early as possible. This will help ensure that the design meets the goals of the organization. This will most often be accomplished by discussing business goals with yours stakeholders. From these discussions, we can deduce Non-Functional Requirements from statements pertaining to business goals. Another approach is to ask pointed questions of your stakeholders using the quality attributes list I just went over. This approach must include explanations as to cost and time related to the quality attributes I just went over. We can't just ask the stakeholder if he or she feels the system needs to be scalable, because the answer will inevitably be yes; of course it does. A better tact would be to ask the stakeholder the number of users expected to use the system initially, what it might grow to in the future, and what the business impact would be if the system was unavailable for an hour or even a day. From answers to these questions, we can deduce the need for scalability and weight this against infrastructure and development cost. The result is non-functional scalability requirements of the system and how we came to this conclusion.

Requirements Definition

- Functional Requirements
  - Ensure analysts provide good requirements
  - Basis for architect, development and QA teams
  - Provide guidance and mentoring to BA's
  - Good functional requirements define WHAT system should do
    - Not HOW it should be implemented
  - If HOW is provided by analyst then this is an opportunity for mentoring
  - Functional requirements are important
    - Basis for design
    - Basis for development
    - Basis for test scenarios
  - Architect is a consumer of the requirements

- Provide support and guidance to BA team
- Architect must understand functional requirements

A secondary role of the solutions architect during Requirements Definition is to ensure that the analysts provide a good set of requirements. This is important because a good set of requirements will be used as the basis for the application architect, development, and QA teams. It's been my experience that quite often business analysts confuse the goal of Functional Requirements, so providing guidance and mentoring is an important part of the architect's job. We won't spend much time describing Functional Requirements, except to say that a good Functional Requirement defines what a function or component of the system should accomplish. It should describe inputs, behaviors, and outputs of a function or component, but not how something should be implemented. How the behaviors are implemented are the responsibility of the application architect and the development team. If the HOW portion is provided by an analyst, then this might be an indication that the analyst needs mentoring. Functional Requirements are important to the software architect because they're used as the basis for the subsystem and component design. They're used by architects to design the solution, developers when building the application, and by quality assurance as the basis to generate test scenarios. The architect is primarily a consumer of the functional requirements, but does provide guidance to the team creating them. He or she must also understand them before design begins.

Requirements Definition

- Architectural Constraints
  - Architectural constraints greatly influence design decisions
  - Constraints impact design choices
  - Constraints come in many flavors
  - Architect identifies constraints

Identifying Architectural Constraints for the solution is important because like Non-Functional Requirements, they can greatly influence your design decisions. I'm including constraints as part of requirements because this is typically where the Architectural Constraints are defined. While these are not really requirements of the solution, they do impact the choices that will be made in design. Architectural Constraints come in many flavors and it's the architect's job to identify and understand them all.

Requirements Definition

- Architectural Constraints
  - Examples:
    - Time
    - Resource
    - Budget
    - Team Skills
    - Deployed infrastructure
    - Standards
      - Architectural
      - Technology
      - Coding

Some examples of constraints might be Time, Resource, Budget, Team Skills, Deployed Infrastructure, and Architectural, Technology, and Coding standards.

Requirements Definition
- **Architectural Constraints**
    - **Come from customers, business and technology**
    - **Required condition of design or implementation**
    - **Architects job is to identify constraints**
        - **Account for them in design**
        - **Account for them in implementation**

Constraints can come from your customers, the business or even technology portions of the organization. They are anything that's dictated as a required condition when designing or implementing the solution. The architect's job is to identify these constraints and make sure that the solution accounts for them during design and implementation.

Design

The architect's role in the project life cycle
- **Design**
    - **Design is inward facing and creative**
    - **Define structures that make up solution**
    - **Documentation is outward facing and communicative**
    - **Two distinct goals**
    - **Design is the most interesting part of project for some people**
    - **Design is creative**

- Design solves complex problems with interesting solutions

Software Design is the mental problem solving process where you create a software solution that meets the needs of the business. I've separated this from documentation because each is a discreet process that solves a different problem. Design is an inward facing and creative process that focuses solely on understanding and defining the solution. The goal of Design is to define the structures that make up the solution. Documentation is outward facing, focusing on communicating the solution externally to an audience. Often the two are performed in unison, but make no mistake - these are independent processes with different goals. For most architects, myself included, this is the most interesting and fun part of the project. This is the part where we're creative. You get to solve complex problems with interesting solutions. This is why developers and architects love their job; it's the problem solving and the creativity that we enjoy most. We all say that we love coding, but in truth coding is hard work and can get very tedious. It's the creative portion we love, the sense of accomplishment and pride we feel when we see our designs realized, and it's working to solve the problem that we truly all love.

Design
- Least expensive time to make mistakes
- Make your mistakes during design
  - Less expensive
- Design is collaborative

- Design is iterative
- Trusted group of colleagues
  - Joint design
  - Architectural review
  - Essential for creating solid designs

Design is the least expensive time to make mistakes, so make them and make them fast. We all make mistakes with our designs; this is a fact. The challenge is to make your mistakes as part of the design process so that they can be found and corrected early on when it's less expensive. Changing a design on paper may cost a few hours, but changing a design once coded can take days, weeks or even months. The further downstream the problems are identified, the higher the cost to correct them. Design is collaborative and iterative so don't get too hung up on making mistakes; you can correct them as part of another iteration. Architects quite often have a trusted group of colleagues, either other architects or developers, so that they can do joint design or review their architectures. This is essential for creating solid designs and finding your mistakes early.

Design
- Vision
  - Design is where we realize your visions true value
  - Vision is the foundation of your design
  - Design is iterative process of decomposition
  - Vision guides the design at every level
  - Make sure your vision is documented

Design starts with a Vision of the solution that you begin formulating at Project Initiation. Your Project Vision will be used throughout the project, but this is where we begin to realize its true value. Your vision will be used as the foundation of the solution architecture. Design is the iterative process of decomposing a solution into progressively smaller parts. Your vision serves as an overarching guide to every level of decomposition. If you didn't take the time to create a vision artifact, now's the time.

Design

- Understand the whole problem
    - Process of understanding the whole problem will never be complete
    - Paradox
        - Must understand whole problem that is changing and evolving
    - Requirements change in every phase of the project
        - Sometimes business changes
        - Sometimes we really don't understand the whole problem
    - Design is iterative
    - Design must anticipate changes
    - Modular designs help mitigate
    - How can I anticipate changes?
        - You can't!
        - Identify risky parts of the solution
        - Design solution to mitigate these risks

- Risky portions often occur at boundaries
- Pay careful attention to portions of the solution that you do not control
    - Treat these as high risk
    - Protect the solution from risky dependencies
    - Insulate your solution from changes in these dependencies

Before one can define the solution, the entire problem domain must be understood. The preceding phases of the life cycle should have helped the architect to gain an understanding of the needs, desires, goals, motivations, and requirements of the problem space. However, it's important to note that the process of understanding the whole will never be complete. This is the paradox we must all embrace. We must understand the whole of a problem that will never be completely understood because it continues to change and evolve over time. Project requirements change in every phase of the project, sometimes because the business changes and sometimes because we find that we really didn't understand the requirements in the first place. Design is an iterative process, whose inputs are ever changing. Our designs must anticipate these changes so that they can accommodate them with as little impact as possible. Creating modular designs that can be changed and replaced over time is one way to address this issue. Now I know what you're thinking, how can I anticipate changes? Well the answer is you can, but you can identify the portions of the solution that are most likely to change and design your solution accordingly. These risky portions of the design often, but not always occur at its boundaries. Pay careful attention to the portions of the system that you do not control. These can be third party integrations or enterprise solutions where you'll have no influence. Treat these interfaces as high risk and take care to protect your design from these dependencies. Insulate the solution from changes in these systems.

Design
- Collaboration
  - Leverage your technical feedback loop
    - This team will help you identify design issues
    - Cultivate these relationships
  - Collaboration fosters ownership and support
    - Advocates, evangelists & voice
    - Investment in solution
    - Collaborative design becomes teams
    - Help provide explanations for design decisions

Collaboration is important in the Design phase for a number of reasons. As I stated before, Design is the least expensive time to make mistakes so make them fast and make them early. Create or leverage your technical feedback loop of trusted architects or developers. These people will provide feedback, suggestions, and ideas that you may have never come up with without their help. They're how you identify issues with the design that you might not see. Cultivate these relationships, they're critical to the success of the project, as well as your own. A secondary benefit to Collaboration is fostering ownership and support. It will important to have developers committed to your design when construction begins. They will be your advocates, evangelists, and your voice on the development team. They'll be more invested in a solution that they helped create. When a team collaborates on a design, it becomes the teams, not yours. Additionally, they'll be able to help provide explanations and background for the decisions made during design.

Design
- Collaboration
  - Small committed design teams are best
  - 3 people works best
  - May collaborate with different people for different parts of the design
    - High level design with one group
    - Detailed design with senior developers

When picking your team, it's critical to only include people that will bring value to the process. Keep these teams small, adding too many people will slow the process down to a crawl. There's no correct number, but I would suggest having no more than 3 people at most involved in any single design session. It may be helpful to have different people collaborate on different parts of the design. You don't have to collaborate with the same people for every part of the system. Sometimes it's best to design the high level portions of the system with one group and then do the more detailed design with senior developers that may be responsible for that part of the solution.

Design
- Collaboration
  - When selecting your design team:
    - Ideal candidates are experienced and senior developers and architects
    - Ideal candidates know how to offer constructive but not critical advice
    - Ideal candidates are not afraid to offer their frank opinion
    - This is not the place to mentor junior developers
    - This is not the place for unconstructive criticism

Here are a few things to keep in mind when selecting your design team. Ideal candidates are experienced and senior developers or architects. Ideal candidates know how to offer constructive, but not critical advice. Ideal candidates are not afraid to offer their frank opinion, but understand that there are many solutions to a given problem, not just their own. This is not the place to mentor junior developers and this is not the place for unconstructive criticism.

Design

- Collaboration
    - Design Sessions:
        - Begin with brainstorming sessions
        - Architect will get everyone up to speed
        - Team must understand the whole problem that is being solved
        - Ideas should not be criticized
        - Identify the best ideas
        - Best ideas are often the synthesis of a few good ideas

Design Sessions with this team initially begin as brainstorming sessions where you and your team throw a bunch of ideas on the wall to see what sticks. If your team does not understand the whole problem, it's your job to get everyone up to speed. This can be done during this meeting or prior, but it's imperative that everyone have a thorough understanding of the problem you're trying to solve in the Design Session. This doesn't mean that everyone has to understand every aspect of the project, it means that your team must understand the whole problem that you're trying to solve in this particular Design Session. This should be a place where ideas are not criticized, but accepted and whose merits are discussed. If you include experienced developers and architects in your group, then you'll not waste much time on impractical decisions. This team understands the problem and is focused on solutions that meet the needs, goals, and motivations of the entire project team. They understand the requirements and the constraints, they're experts in business and technical domains. These sessions should be focused on identifying the best ideas the group has to offer and making them better. The goal of the Design Session is to hear a number of good ideas, looking for the best. Often the best solution is the synthesis of a few good ideas. This process is invaluable and a necessary part of Design.

Design

- Documentation
    - Design identifies structures
    - Views communicate structures to an audience
    - Documentation communicates solution externally to an audience
    - Views are representations of design to a particular audience
        - Some views target business
        - Some views target technical
        - Some views target both
    - No right or wrong number of views
    - View represents single perspective
    - Views are windows into your design
    - No single viewpoint represents entire solution

Documentation is the final step in the Design Phase, but it's often performed simultaneously with Design. One of the main goals of the Design process was to identify all the structures that make up the solution. Once these structures are identified, the next step is to create views that effectively communicate these structures to an audience. Documenting a solution focuses on communicating the solution externally to an audience. Views are representations of the design created to communicate information to a particular audience. Some views will target business stakeholders, some will target technical, and some will target both. There is no right or wrong number of views to communicate your solution; this is entirely dependent on what you're attempting to communicate and to whom. Each view represents a single perspective of the solution to that audience. We'll discuss views in more detail in module 4, but for now think of them as windows into your design. Each provided different viewpoint where no single view represents the entire solution.

Construction

The architect's role in the project life cycle
- Construction
  - Technical team lead
  - Guide the development team
  - Assist with resource planning
  - Fill technical gaps

The architect very actively participates in the Construction phase of the project as a technical team lead, guiding the development team, and assisting the project manager with resource planning. He or she is available to fill any technical gaps discovered during construction.

Construction

- Project Management
    - Technical project manager
    - Organize project into logical segments
    - Resource planning
    - Fills knowledge gap
    - Train team

Rarely does an architect hand off their design to a development team. He or she quite often remains on the project as a sort of technical project manager, organizing the project into logical segments that can be worked on independently and managed by the project manager. In this role, he helps the project manager to plan the project and to assign resources in the most effective manner. While logically segmenting the team is very effective for managing the project, it does leave a gap in the understanding of the solution as a whole. Each of the independent teams will understand the portion they're responsible for, but not necessarily all aspects of the entire solution. The architect may initially be the only person on that team that has knowledge of all components that make up the solution and how the interoperate. This often results in the architect filling this knowledge gap until the team is up to speed. It will be the architect's responsibility to perform the necessary training to get the team up to speed.

Construction

- Insulate your development team

- Insulates development team from meeting overload
- Act as technical team representative
- Communicate decisions

The architect should attempt to insulate the development team from meeting overload. One unfortunate result of working on a large team in the enterprise is that even small decisions require large meetings with lots of debate that steal large blocks of time from your day. Often developers don't get much from attending these meetings as they only really need to know the result of the meeting and not how a decision was arrived at. Sometimes it can even cause frustration on your team because they feel like there's just no time for coding. Insulate your team from these time syncs and act as the team representative. Your team will appreciate it and be more productive because they're spending these extra hours doing what they like to do without interruption. It will be your job to communicate any decisions made during the meeting, but this can typically occur in a short email or a 15 minute impromptu meeting that doesn't impact their work.

Construction
- Design Validation
  - Stay one step ahead of development effort
  - Reviews functional requirements
  - Provide technical direction
  - Architectural pivots
  - Project scope negotiation
  - Reacts to changes

The architect continues to validate the design even after construction has begun, making every effort to stay one step ahead of the development effort. He or she will continue to review the functional requirements with the business analysts and business looking for any holes in the design, making sure that assumptions made at earlier phases in the project still hold true. These reviews serve as a sort of design validation that occurs as part of the current project iteration. When the architect or someone on the development team discovers something that could impact the design, it's up to the architect to provide direction to the team. This could result in a design pivot where the team must scramble to correct whatever flaw was discovered. The architect would lead this effort collaboratively with the development team. This could also lead to project scope negotiation with the business, which the architect would also lead. The architect provides guidance and helps the team to react to changes or obstacles discovered during construction.

Construction

- Development Environment
    - Establish development environment
    - Environment should reflect production
    - Separate from qa

Before coding begins, the architect should identify the Development Environment or make sure one is created if one doesn't exist. Having a Development Environment will be required even if working with only a small team. This environment should reflect the same number of physical tiers that will be deployed in production. This environment should be separate from the Quality Assurance Environment we'll discuss in the next section.

Construction

- Tools Technologies & Standards
  - Development IDE
  - Programming Language
  - Unit Testing requirements
  - Change Management practices
  - Source code repository
  - Coding Standards
  - Establish these standards if they don't exist

The architect should identify the Tools, Technologies, and Standards that the team should use. These include Development IDE, Programming Language, Unit Testing requirements, Change Management practices, Source code repository, and even Coding Standards. In most cases your organization will already have an established set of Tools, Technologies, and Standards in place, but if not, then it's the architect's job to establish these standards.

Construction

- Code Reviews
  - Code review should be a integral part of your process
  - Required of every team member
  - Open/team code reviews
  - Goals:
    - Verify design conformance
    - Insure code quality

- Provide platform for developer to show work
- Provide positive feedback
- Motivate
- Constructive criticism
- Help team members grow
- Train junior members
- Educate entire team on solution
- Positive experience

The last item I'd like to touch on is Code Review. Code Reviews should be an integral part of your development process and required of every member on your team, including yourself. Code Reviews provide a number of benefits; they aren't just about ensuring code quality. On my projects, I require open code reviews that anyone on the team may attend. My primary goal is to verify that the design is being conformed to and to ensure code quality; however, my secondary goal is to provide a platform for the developer to show his or her work to the team. This may be his or her only opportunity to receive positive feedback for all their hard work and effort. It's your job as an architect to provide the platform and to facilitate these meetings. The goal of Code Reviews is not to constrain the creativity of the development team. The positive feedback they'll get will help motivate your team to continue to strive for high quality. If issues are uncovered during the walkthrough then they should be identified constructively and noted for followup. It will be up to you to make sure that this is a positive process that helps your team members grow. Code Reviews also provide training benefits for the team and even the architect. They'll help to train junior developers by exposing them to more advanced coding practices. Code Reviews will also help to educate your team on portions of the project that they may not be working on. Code Reviews are not necessarily performed by the architect. They may be performed by senior developers on your team or could even be team evaluations. The important thing here is to keep them positive.

Testing

The architect's role in the project life cycle
- Testing
  - Quality assurance testing
  - Performance testing

The Testing phase of the project can be separated into two categories: quality assurance testing and performance testing.
Testing
- Quality Assurance Testing
  - Supportive Role
  - Help testers understand requirements
  - Help translate requirements into test cases
  - Make sure quality assurance environment exists
  - Make sure quality assurance environment is being utilized
  - Support development team
    - Advice

- Strategies
- Design changes

Let's first address Quality Assurance Testing. The architect's role with respect to Quality Assurance Testing is primarily supportive. He or she should be available to help the Quality Assurance Team or Business Analyst Team understand how functional requirements have been met by the application being constructed. He or she may also help translate business requirements into testable use cases. The architect plays an active role in making sure that a quality assurance environment exists and is being utilized. The environment should be planned from the onset of the project and considered as important as your development environment. It's the job of the architect to make sure that this environment exists and that it's being used. When design-related issues are uncovered as a result of Quality Assurance Testing, it's the job of the architect to assist the development team in correcting these issues if his help is needed. Assisting will primarily be in the form of Advice, Strategies, and even Design changes if needed.

Testing

- Performance Testing
  - Architect is actively involved
  - Architect decides if performance testing is necessary for project
  - Understand your quality constraints
  - When performance testing is necessary
    - Support team

- Guide team
- Architect may act as project manager for performance team
- Identify environment
- Identify performance testing tools

Performance Testing is an area where the architect is very actively involved. Performance Testing is a very costly and time consuming process that requires a team with specialized knowledge to execute effectively. The architect's first goal is to make the decision whether or not Performance Testing is necessary for his or her project. After all, not every project will need to scale out to hundreds or thousands of users, so Performance Testing is not always necessary. To make this determination, the architect should evaluate the performance-related quality attributes of the project. He or she should also have an idea of the number of users that the application will need to support from the onset and what the future expectations will be. From this information, he or she can make the decision as to whether performance testing is necessary. Once the architect decides that performance testing is necessary, then it is his or her job to work as a technical team lead, supporting and guiding the performance team. Because performance testing is such a time consuming task, it's typically spun up as a separate project, performed by a team that has specialized knowledge in performance testing. This team is often assigned a project manager, but when one is not assigned, the job may fall to you as the architect. If this is the case, the architect's first objective will be to identify the test environment and performance testing tools to be utilized. This environment should not be the same as the one we identified for Quality Assurance Testing. If your organization has a performance testing environment, then this will be your obvious choice. If not, then your team's first goal is to create an environment that closely matches production and decide which testing tools should be utilized.

Testing

- Performance Testing
    - Guidance
        - Acceptance criteria
        - Test design
        - Analyze test results
    - Performance related recommendations
    - React to findings
    - Modify architecture if needed
    - Prototype
    - Evaluate

The architect will also provide guidance with regard to performance acceptance criteria, test design, and analyzing the test cases. If any performance-related issues are identified, the architect in collaboration with the testing team will make performance-related recommendations back to the project team. If any architecturally significant issues are identified, then the architect may have to make changes to his or her design. Often these changes will be prototyped by the performance team to evaluate improvements before taking these recommendations to the project team to implement.

Implementation

The architect's role in the project life cycle
- Implementation
  - Coordinate deployment
    - Change management team
    - Infrastructure team

The architect's role during implementation is to help coordinate deployment with the change management and infrastructure teams.

Implementation
- Coordinate with Infrastructure Team
  - New or existing infrastructure?
  - Existing infrastructure should be identified as an architectural constraint
  - New environment
    - Collaborate with infrastructure
    - Physical tier design
  - Implementation considerations
    - Availability
    - Interoperability
    - Performance
    - Reliability
    - Scalability
    - Security
  - Non-functional run-time attributes may greatly impact implementation
  - Heath Check
  - Performance Monitors

As part of the Design phase, the architect collaborates with the infrastructure team to determine if the solution should reside on new or existing infrastructure. In many cases, the direction of the organization will be to deploy to an existing environment. If this is the case, then this should be identified as an architectural constraint during the Requirements phase. When a new environment is required, the software architect will work closely with the infrastructure team to design the proper environment. In either case, the software architect will often produce a physical tier design as part of his or her design deliverables. This artifact identifies all tiers and communication requirements of the solution. This information will help the infrastructure team to understand the types of servers and communication protocols required. The architect will consider many of the non-functional runtime attributes, like Availability, Interoperability, Performance, Reliability, Scalability, and Security, when creating this design. These attributes will greatly impact the choices that are made when either creating or leveraging an existing environment. All infrastructure-related decisions should have been made long before this phase of the project. At this point in the process, the architect's job is to help coordinate deployment with the infrastructure team. They will need to be aware that the solution is being deployed and that Health Checks and Performance Monitors should be in place.

Implementation

- **Coordinate with Change Management Team**

- Collaborate, mentor & guide change management team
- 3 Main areas of concern:
  - Source code management
  - Build management
  - Deployment
- Architect must ensure source control is in place
- Architect must ensure automated build process is in place
- Coordinate solution deployment to production
- Architect must ensure automated deployments are in place
- Architect remains available for troubleshooting if needed

In most organizations, there'll be a separate Change Management Group assigned to managing builds and deployments for your team. Your job as an architect is to collaborate, mentor, and guide this team. There are 3 main areas of change management that the architect should be concerned with: Source code management, Build management, and Deployment. Source code management is standard practice in most organizations. Presumably everyone taking this book understands the benefits of source control so I'm not going to spend any time discussing its merits. There are many great source control solutions available, many of which are free, so if your organization doesn't have source control in place, then it's up to you as the architect to make sure one is implemented. Automated build processes are also standard practice in most organizations. Automating your build process provides for a consistent and repeatable process that will improve product quality and help ensure consistency with your deployments. Automated builds are quite often combined with automated unit testing and deployment, which further help to improve product quality and productivity. If your organization has not invested the time in implementing an automated build process, then you as the architect should lead this charge. Coordinating the deployment of the solution into your production environment with change management and infrastructure will be critical of the success of your project. Automated deployments will help to ensure consistency in the deployment process. So if your organization has not already embraced automated deployments, then it will be up to you as the architect to make sure this happens. Once the solution is implemented in production, the architect and development teams remain available for troubleshooting should problems arise, but the daily health and management of the solution quite often fall to other teams.

Summary

The architect's role in the project life cycle
- Summary
  - Duties of the software architect in each phase of the project

- Effective architects don't just design solutions
- Architects play an important role from initiation through implementation
- Active participants in each and every phase of the project
- May be a bit daunting
- Representation of the duties performed
- Architect role is very opaque
- Varies between organizations
- Many organizations don't have clearly defined roles for the architect
- Up to you to define your role in the organisation

In this module we covered all the phases of a typical project and what effective architects do in each phase. We covered a lot of material primarily focusing on the duties of the software architect in each phase of the project. I hope I demonstrated that effective architects don't just design a solution and throw it over the fence to the development team to implement, they play an important role in the project from initiation to implementation. They're active participants in each and every phase playing a vital role in keeping the project moving towards successful completion. Now I understand that this list may be a bit daunting to you if you're new to the role or just considering becoming an architect. Understand that the duties I outlined in this module are not hard and fast rules defining what each and every architect does in every organization, they're meant to be a representation of the duties an architect performs as part of his or her job in the enterprise. You'll find that the architect role is very opaque and that there are many differences between organizations and even between architects in the same organization. You'll find that in some organizations, architects really do only participate in Design; in some organizations, they participate in Design through Construction phases; and yet others, they do participate in all phases. The reason for this is that many organizations don't have clearly defined roles for the architect. I would even go a bit further and say that many organizations don't even really understand what architects should be doing; they just know that they need a senior technical person to work with the development team that helps deliver projects. This means that it's often left to you to help define your role and help educate your organization on what you should be doing. How you as an architect can bring leadership and vision to your organization. This module was intended to help give you a head start, a roadmap if you will into understanding what truly effective architects do for their organizations and how you too can become a truly effective architect.

Designing the Solution

Introduction

This is the module, Designing the Solution. In the previous module, we discussed the design phase as one of the many phases of a project and the architect's role during that phase.

Designing the Solution
- Design phase
  - Design
  - Document
- Two halves
  - Design
  - Communicating the design
- Software architecture
  - What are software architecture & detailed design?
  - Goals
  - How are they different?
  - Who should perform them?
  - The role of architecture in an agile world

In this module, we're going to focus solely on the Design phase and how to Design and Document a solution. These are two of the most important responsibilities of the architect so I want to spend some time discussing them in detail, making this part of the book as practical as possible. I separated this module into two halves. The first concentrates on Design and the second on Communicating your design. The Design section begins with software architecture. In this section, we'll first spend some time defining what software architecture & detailed design are, their goals, how they're different, and who should perform them. We'll discuss the role of architecture in the agile world and how many of the concepts that we've already covered can be applied when using agile methodologies. We'll then spend some time discussing architectural design approaches.

Designing the Solution

- Approach to Architectural Design
  - Two fundamental approaches
    - Top-down
    - Bottom-up
    - Which is the right choice?
- Architectural Design Process
  - Design Considerations
  - Design process step by step
  - Prototypes
  - Architectural Patterns
  - When to use them

We'll cover the two fundamental approaches to Design, Top-down and Bottom-up, and which is the right choice. We'll then cover the Architectural Design Process in detail, first with Design Considerations and then I'll walk you through the Design Process step by step. To finish up the Design section, we'll review Prototypes, Architectural Patterns, and when to use them.

Designing the Solution

- Communicating the Solution
  - 3 Main Objectives

- Documentation standards
- What are views?
  - 4+1 architectural view model
  - Views and Beyond
- Views & Beyond in practice
  - Examples
    - Module View
    - Component-and-Connector View
    - Allocation Views

We'll then begin the second half of the module by discussing how to Communicate your Solution. We'll cover the 3 Main Objectives of architectural documentation and then we'll discuss documentation standards. From there I'll answer the question what are views and discuss how they're utilized in the 4+1 architectural view and the Views and Beyond approaches. We'll wrap up the module with Views & Beyond in practice. In this section, I'll discuss the Views & Beyond approach and provide examples of how to apply this approach in the real world. I'll provide a number of examples of Module, Component-and-Connector, and Allocation Views. Now let's get started.

Software Architecture

So What is Software Architecture? Let's begin by defining the term Software Architecture. The book Software Engineering in Practice (3rd Edition) defines Software Architecture as, "The software architecture of a system is the set of structures needed to reason about the system, which comprise of software elements, relations among them, and properties of both. " I really like this definition because it's concise, it clearly identifies what we're attempting to achieve with the architecture. Software Architecture

- What is Software Architecture?
    - A set of structures that communicate the goals of the solution
    - Singular task: to identify the structures, their elements, and the relationships between them
    - Properties and behaviors must be identified
    - Architecture must define publicly visible properties that identify how elements relate and interact with each other
    - Architecture must have 4 attributes
        - Elements
        - Relations
        - Properties
        - Behavior
    - The architecture need only contain the portions of the system that are architecturally significant
    - Design only enough for the team to begin coding or to perform detailed design

We're attempting to define a set of structures that communicate the goals of the solution. The text further breaks down the definition by stating, "A structure is simply a set of elements held together by a relation. " So the architecture has a singular task: to identify the structures, their elements, and the relationships between them. A secondary, yet equally important message, is that properties and behaviors must be identified. Here, the authors are talking about externally visible properties that are interfaces. That is to say the architecture must define publicly visible properties that identify how elements relate and interact with each other. The interaction between elements expresses their behavior. In a nutshell, our architecture must have 4 attributes. It must contain Elements, Relations, Properties, and Behavior. At this point, you may be saying to yourself, 'This sure is a lot of detail for us to capture in the limited amount of time we have on that typical project. ' The text addresses this by stating: "A structure is architectural if it supports reasoning about the system and the system's properties. " This means that the architecture need only contain the portions of the system that are architecturally significant. It's the job of the architect to decide which structure should be included and to what degree. It's not necessary to include commonly understood areas of the solution. A general rule that many architects follow is, "Design only enough for the team to begin coding or to perform detailed design. " This will vary based on the team size, experience, and relationship, but it's the architect's job to know when enough is enough.

Software Architecture
- What is Software Architecture?
  - The architecture not only defines the structures of the solution but provides structure to your project

- Guiding the project through all phases
- Providing constraints for the team to work within
- Directing toward successful completion
- Architects Primary Objective
  - Provide architecturally significant structures which are made up of: elements, relations, properties and behaviors
  - Create a blueprint that guides and shapes the implementation with regard to the pieces that are the most difficult and costly to change

I'd like to take the text definition one step further, reading between the lines, and state, "The architecture not only defines the structures of the solution but provides structure to your project. " The architecture provides structure by guiding the project through all phases, providing constraints for the team to work within, and directing it toward a successful completion. Without this structure, the choices your development team will be faced with can be daunting. Architects provide boundaries in the form of architecture that provides structure and parameters for the development team to work within. Picture the architecture as a sort of pinball machine, where your project is the ball bouncing all around the game, hitting bumpers on all sides and flippers protecting the drain at the bottom of the game. The bumpers are the constraints that the architecture enforces; each put there intentionally to guide the team's decisions during construction; each put in place to mitigate risk by defining a vision with clear goals expressed as the architecture and implemented in code. I think of the flippers at the bottom as the architect protecting the project from the drain by keeping the ball moving in the right direction whenever any obstacle or challenge is encountered. Now for those of you much younger than myself, who don't know what a pinball machine is, a pinball machine is basically a coin operated arcade game where you bounce a steel ball all over the playing field, trying to acquire as many points as possible. Yeah, I know that doesn't sound like much fun compared to what's available now, but that was state of the art gaming for us back then. Now getting back to architecture, the architect's Primary Objective is to provide the architecturally significant structures, which are made up of elements, relations, properties, and behaviors. The objective is not to define every portion of the system to the lowest level of detail. The objective is to create a blueprint that guides and shapes the implementation with regard to the pieces that are the most difficult and costly to change. The architect must weigh both Functional and Non-Functional Requirements, as well as the architectural constraints when creating this blueprint. So now that we have what I hope is a clear definition of what an architecture is, let's talk a bit about the differences between architectural design and what is commonly referred to detailed design.

Software Architecture

- What is detailed design?
  - No clear delineation as to where architectural design ends and detailed design begins
  - Lines are not only blurred they move depending on many factors
  - Architecturally significant design choices
    - System wide impact
    - Meet the non-functional requirements
    - Guide downstream design activities
  - Design choices that focus on implementation are non-architectural
  - Design is the process of serially decomposing the whole into its many constituent parts
  - Architectural design is performed until it reaches the point where the development team can begin their work
    - Development team can design individual modules, classes or even begin coding
    - Granularity is dependent not on the architect, or even the project, but on the development team

To begin, I'd first like to point out that there's no real clear delineation as to where architectural design ends and detailed design begins. I'd even go further and say that the lines are not only blurred, but they move depending on many factors. With that said, we do have some guiding principles that will help us determine what should be included in our architectural designs. Architecturally significant design choices are those that have system wide impacts on your solution and its ability to meet the non-functional requirements. They're the choices that guide downstream design activities toward meeting non-functional requirements. Design choices that focus on implementation are non-architectural. Design is the process of serially decomposing the whole into many constituent parts. Now I'm not talking about creating UML diagrams or any form of artifact at this point, I'm focusing solely on the design process. This is the process I outlined in the Design phase of the project and is traditionally performed collaboratively using a white board or note cards to capture ideas. The Architectural Design Process is performed until it reaches a point where the development team can begin their work. By work, I mean they can further design individual modules, classes or even begin coding. This means that the granularity is dependent not on the architect or even the project, but on the development team. Now let me take a moment for that to sink in. If you have a very senior development team, then perhaps just a few simple diagrams on a white board are all that's needed. If your development team is made up of primarily junior developers, then class, sequence, and activity diagrams might be required.

Software Architecture

- What is detailed design?
    - It is not the job of the architect to design every aspect of the solution
    - Development team often has more experience in certain technical domains
    - It is the architects job to:
        - Understand the problem area and identify where the solution should fit within the organization
        - Understand what technologies are best suited to the project
        - Provide structure to the development team with an eye toward meeting the functional, non-functional and business goals of the project
        - Decide when enough is enough –the rest is non-architectural/detailed design

It's not the job of the architect to design every aspect of the solution. The development team will have much to contribute and quite often has more experience in certain technical domains. It's the architect's job to understand the problem area and identify where the solution should fit within the organization, what technologies are best suited to the project, and provide structure to the development team with an eye toward meeting the functional, non-functional, and business goals of the project. It will be up to you as the architect to decide when enough is enough. Design isn't a step that's performed, and once complete, it's never to be addressed again.

Software Architecture

- What is detailed design?
    - Design is evolutionary and iterative
    - Architectural design focuses on the pieces of the solution that are difficult and costly to change
    - Design continues long after architectural design is complete
    - Design is only completed when the project is delivered
    - Development team will continue to make implementation decisions throughout the project life cycle
    - Guided by the architectural design that preceded it

Design is an evolutionary and iterative process that begins with architectural design and progressively moves to more and more detailed design as the team moves closer to implementation. The architectural design focuses on the pieces of the solution that are difficult and costly to change. However, design continues long after the architectural design is complete. I'd even venture to say that the design is only complete when the project is delivered. The development team will continue to make implementation decisions throughout the project life cycle. These design decisions are within the context of the problem at hand and guided by the architectural design that preceded it. This doesn't imply that the architectural design never changes, it sometimes does, but when it does, the impact is often system-wide and painful.

Software Architecture

- How are they different?
- Design process is the same
- Context or scope is the differentiator
- When creating your architectural design it should contain :
    - Structures and elements, that once defined, should rarely change
    - When they do it is extremely painful
- High-level architecture identifies all the top level elements and how they interact
- Detailed design begins with the high-level architecture and continues to fill in the implementation details within each of these elements
- Design process continues throughout the life of the project and only ends with the project's completion

So how is architectural design different from detailed software design? I realize that I haven't given you a clear delineation point, but I'd venture to say that there really isn't one. The design process is the same if you're performing architectural design or detailed design, it's the context or scope that's the differentiator. A simple rule that you can follow is that when creating your architectural design, it should contain the structures and elements that once defined, should rarely change, and when they do it's extremely painful. This is commonly referred to as the high level architecture, which will be used as the basis for more detailed designs that address the implementation. So to put it very simply, the high-level architecture identifies all the top-level elements and how they interact. Detailed design begins with the high-level architecture and continues to fill in the implementation details within each of these elements. The Design process continues throughout the life of the project and only ends with the project's completion.

Software Architecture

- So who does the detailed system design?
  - It depends…
  - Solutions architect is responsible for creating the overall architectural design
  - Application architect is responsible for the more detailed design and implementation choices
  - You may be both the solution and the application architect
  - When separate roles, the delineation point will be more explicit
  - Where you are both the solution architect and the application architect, it will get blurred

- Distinction is important because each task addresses separate concerns of the project

So who does the detailed system design? That's a good question and yet another one where I'll answer - It depends. I told you at the beginning of this book, get used to ambiguity, didn't I? Quite obviously it's your job as a solutions architect to perform the architectural design; however, depending on the team, project or even methodology your team is using, it may be left up to you to create the detailed design as well. The detailed system design is traditionally the responsibility of the application architect or senior members of the development team. Like architectural design, this process is often collaborative and performed on a white board or using note cards. This is where I'd like to tie the book back to the first module, where I introduced the concept of solutions architects and application architects. The solutions architect is responsible for creating the overall architectural design and the application architect is responsible for the more detailed design and implementation choices. Now here's where it gets a bit confusing. In many organizations, this is the same person, this person is you. You may be both the solution and the application architect. Now in organizations where there are separate roles, the delineation point will be more explicit because you must each agree on where your responsibilities lie, but in the case where you're both the solution architect and the application architect, it will definitely get blurred. The distinction is still important because each addresses separate concerns of the project. Remember, this is a sequential process where the focus of the architectural design is on the system as a whole. It's an abstraction that identifies major components, their externally visible properties, and relationships.

Software Architecture

- So who does the detailed system design?
    - Must force yourself to wear two hats and approach each task as discrete units of work, each with different goals
    - Application architect or lead developer performs detailed design
    - Sometimes that is you

The architectural design provides a basis for not only detailed design, but creates a common language, which all stakeholders can use to communicate about their responsibilities and goals. Because of this, you must force yourself to wear two hats and approach each task as discrete units of work, each with different goals. So to answer the question, 'Who does the detail design? ' It's the application architect or lead developer, but sometimes that's you.

Software Architecture

- The role of architecture in an agile world
    - Most, if not all, of the concepts I have outlined still apply
    - On agile teams the architect is most likely a member of the development team

- Architect's qualities are usually present in someone on your team, regardless of title
- When forming teams only a few individuals emerge as leaders
  - Architect asserting his or her role on the project
  - Architect is a role not necessarily a title
- Each phase that I outlined happens on every project no matter what methodology is used
- Iterative and evolving architecture IS an agile approach
- Architects must design solutions that insulate design choices from change
- Approaching design as iterative and evolving helps us to react when we need to

I want to take a moment to address architecture in an agile development environment. You may be thinking to yourself, 'Where does architecture fit? ' if my team uses an agile development methodology? I believe that most, if not all of the concepts I've outlined, still apply. Maybe even more so on an agile team where the architect is most likely a member of the development team. One of the topics in module 1 was, 'Who is a software architect? ' In this section I described an architect's qualities and was careful to point out that these qualities are usually present in someone on your team regardless of the title. This is quite often the case on an agile team. I don't subscribe to the theory that teams are self organized; this implies that the entire team decides who does what on a project and this is most certainly never the case. I believe that collaboration is key and an important consideration for any leader; however, in the formation of teams, there are usually only a few individuals at most that emerge as leaders. These leaders help to organize the team, making decisions regarding design, work assignments, and individual roles. Perhaps you can argue this is self-organizing, but I believe this is in fact the architect asserting his or her role on the project. Remember that the architect role is not necessarily a title. In module 2, I outlined the role of the architect in each phase of the project, but I didn't mention methodology or order. I believe that each phase that I outlined happens on every project no matter what methodology is used. They may happen in a different order than I presented and they may not happen sequentially, but make no mistake they all will happen. In an agile environment, many of these phases are traditionally done as part of an iteration. One notable exception is the Initiation Phase. This happens long before sprint planning even begins and is sometimes referred to as iteration 0. This is a crucial step because this is where the architect begins to form his or her vision for the solution and where important questions as to scope, cost, scheduling, and even strategy are addressed. These insights provide value and direction to each iteration. Lastly, with regard to design, we've discussed the approach to design as an iterative and evolving process. This is unabashedly an agile approach. The notion that requirements, business goals, and even project motivation change is a fact and the belief that our designs will not be effected is a fallacy. As architects, we must design solutions that insulate our design choices from change. We must make choices that allow us to pivot when necessary; however, this doesn't require us to make all our design choices up front. Approaching design both architectural and detailed system level as iterative and evolving helps us to react when we need to. Approaching architecture in this manner allows us to not only adapt, but to build better solution and fit squarely into agile approaches.

Approach to Architectural Design

Approach to Architectural Design
- Large systems are extremely complex and difficult to comprehend in their entirety
- Separate large problem domains into manageable pieces
- Abstract and encapsulate the complexities of the problem at hand
- Many approaches to design
- Two fundamental approaches to design and their benefits
  - Top-down
  - Bottom-up
- Referred to by many names

- Up-front vs evolutionary design
- Decomposition vs composition
- Planned design vs emergent design

Large systems are extremely complex and difficult to comprehend in their entirety. One goal of design is to provide a mechanism for narrowing the scope of what must be understood. The separation of large problem domains into manageable pieces that can be comprehended in their entirety is one of the goals of design. Design seeks to abstract and encapsulate the complexities of the problem at hand into something comprehensible. There are many approaches to design and volumes of information on the internet and in books that discuss best practices on recommended approaches to design. I'm not going to attempt to provide a comprehensive list of design methodologies comparing and contrasting each of them. What I'd like to do in this section is to discuss two fundamental approaches to design and their benefits. I'm not going to attempt to convince you that one is better or more effective than the other, because the truth is each is a tool that serves a different purpose. It's up to the practitioner, you, to decide what is the best tool for the job. The two fundamental approaches to design that I'd like to discuss are Top-down and Bottom-up design. They come in a wide variety of flavors and are referred to by many names like up-front vs evolutionary design, decomposition vs composition, planned design vs emergent design.

Approach to Architectural Design

- Top-down
  - Highest level of abstraction, progressively work downward
- Bottom-up
  - Focus on the components that makeup the solution, working upward
- All have common objectives
  - Create a set of common terms that can be used to facilitate communications
  - Provide a representation of functional components
  - Create a model that facilitates the partitioning of the problem domain

While there are many names, there are two fundamental concepts that I'm going to refer to as top-down and bottom-up design. Top-down design looks at the solution from the highest level of abstraction and then progressively works it downward, providing more and more detail. Bottom-up has an opposite approach where we focus on the components that make up the solution, working upward to assemble them into the whole. No matter what technique we use, they all have common objectives. They seek to create a set of common terms that can be used to facilitate communications between stakeholders on the team. They seek to provide a representation of functional components, their interfaces and relationships, and they seek to create a model that facilitates the partitioning of the problem domain. No matter what approach you choose, these three primary objectives will be the goal.

Approach to Architectural Design
- Top-down
  - Traditional approach
  - Break down the system into a series of components
  - Begins at the highest level of detail
  - Performed iteratively
  - Series of sequential decomposition exercises
  - Series of black boxes, interfaces and relationships
  - Basis for implementation choices
  - Common in the enterprise
  - Most effective when the problem domain is well understood
  - Architect focuses on the larger issues up front

The top-down approach design is the traditional approach that many architects and developers are familiar with. They goal of the top-down approach is to break down the system into a series of components with inputs and outputs. As the name implies, the designer starts at the highest level of detail and progressively refines it into lower and lower levels of detail. This process is performed iteratively as a series of sequential decomposition exercises. The top-down approach starts with the big picture and breaks it down into smaller and smaller components. In the end, the design identifies a series of black boxes, interfaces, and relationships between them. These structures are used as the basis for implementation choices. The top-down approach is quite common in the enterprise where there are often many large projects with big teams. It's most effective when the problem domain is well understood with clear requirements and objectives. When using the top-down approach, the architect focuses on the larger issues up front, leaving the more tactical decisions to the developers.

Approach to Architectural Design

- Top-down benefits
    - Effective on both large and small projects
    - Provides a logical and systematic approach
    - Lends itself to system partitioning
    - Helps to reduces size, scope and complexity of each module
    - Works for both functional and object oriented design

There are several benefits to this approach. Top-down design can be very effective on both large and small teams. Top-down design provides a logical and systematic approach, which is beneficial when creating complex systems. When scaling your process to large teams and complex systems, the approach requires a systematic process to make sure everything is accounted for and that your team is organized properly. Top-down design lends itself to system partitioning and the separation of responsibilities between components. Top-down design helps to reduce size, scope, and complexity of each module, which is beneficial for system partitioning, separation of responsibilities, and resource allocation.

Top-down design works with both functional and object-oriented design approaches.
Approach to Architectural Design

- Top-down drawbacks
  - Requires an in depth understanding of problem domain
  - Partitioning doesn't facilitate reuse
  - Sometimes leads to ivory tower architecture
  - Design flaws can sometimes ripple up to the highest layers

I don't want to paint too rosy a picture though, there are some drawbacks as well. Top-down design requires an in depth understanding of the problem domain. Most of you taking this book have probably been developing software for a number of years now, so I'm sure it's not any surprise to you to know that end users rarely know what they want. This makes it extremely difficult to have a complete understanding of the entire problem domain at the beginning of the project. While partitioning is great for organizing your teams, it doesn't facilitate reuse. Teams are traditionally organized by the subsystem or module, which is extremely efficient because each can run as a separate project. However, the challenge you run into is with code reuse and knowledge sharing between the teams, because each team functions independently of the other. Top-down sometimes leads to ivory tower architectures as well, where the architect performs the design and hands it off to the development team to implement. When the requirements change and they always do, the design will need to adapt, and if the architect isn't engaged, then this can cause delays, or worse yet, programmers may start to work around the design. Ivory tower architecture is bad for the project team, and yes, even the architect. Lastly, if design flaws are found during implementation, the impact can sometimes ripple up to the highest layers. This may cause a significant amount of work to both the architect and development team. Now let's move on to bottom-up design.

Approach to Architectural Design
- Bottom-up
    - Process of defining the system in small parts
    - Like assembling Legos
    - Where concept of emergent architecture is founded
    - Typically encountered when using an agile development methodology
    - More common than top-down?
    - Is there an architecture when you chose bottom-up?
    - As the project progresses the architecture really does emerge...eventually

The bottom-up approach, as its name also implies, is the process of defining the system in small parts or components and then assembling them together to create the entire system. I once read, but can't recall where, that bottom-up design is like assembling a bunch of Legos. Each component is like a Lego that, once designed, can be composed into higher and higher levels. Bottom-up design is where the concept of emergent architecture is founded. When using a bottom-up design approach, the architecture emerges from the composition of its component parts. This bottom-up design approach is typically encountered when using an agile development methodology. Some might even argue that this approach is more common than top-down because on small projects and teams where there's no formal architect design, the architecture really does emerge as the project progresses. Some might also argue that when using bottom-up design techniques, there really isn't an architecture, because we're designing the pieces, not a blueprint of the system as a whole. To me this argument does have merit, but I personally don't subscribe to it in its entirety. I do believe that many solutions are created this way initially. As a matter of fact, I've worked on many projects that begin this way; however, as the project progresses, the architecture really does emerge eventually. It emerges through many iterations of refactorings and aha moments. At this point, I may be getting a little bit ahead of myself so let me back up and get back to bottom-up design.

Approach to Architectural Design
- Bottom-up advantages
  - Allows a team to begin coding and testing early
  - Simplicity
  - Promotes code reuse
  - Promotes the use of continuous integration and unit testing

Bottom-up design has many advantages over top-down. Bottom-up design allows a team to begin coding and testing early without a long period of requirements definition. A complete understanding of the problem domain isn't required because the team is focused on delivering a single piece at a time. Simplicity is often promoted as a benefit of bottom-up design. Since the team only builds what they need, the complexity of the design is reduced. When something is needed it will be designed, but until that time it's not even a consideration. Bottom-up design promotes code reuse. Because the team is designing and building one component at a time, they know where and when code reuse is an option. Bottom-up design promotes the use of continuous integration and unit testing. Both are beneficial and promote automation, high quality, and rapid deployment. This doesn't imply that top-down design can't utilize these techniques, but with bottom-up design, these really are required for success, especially as your team grows.

Approach to Architectural Design
- Bottom-up disadvantages
  - Can become difficult to maintain
  - Benefits of code reuse are eliminated or at least delayed as the team grows
  - Design flaws can ripple throughout the entire solution

Bottom-up also has some disadvantages too. As the system grows in complexity, it can become difficult to maintain because there was no consideration as to how subsystems and modules would interoperate. The resulting system may function, but without a consistent architecture it will appear coupled together, becoming more and more difficult to maintain and extend over time.

Cumulative changes to a system like this will cause it to further deteriorate, compounding these issues. At the onset of the project, these may not seem like serious concerns, but remember - the majority of the costs of a solution are the long-term maintenance costs, not the initial development costs. Another disadvantage of bottom-up design is that many of the benefits of code reuse are eliminated or at least delayed as the team grows. Let me explain. While teams grow and begin to design and implement components concurrently, their interaction and collaboration suffers or becomes non-existent. Because each team begins to work independently, the benefit of a code reuse begins to wane or requires a tremendous amount of refactoring. While this isn't a disadvantage when working with a small team, you will find that most projects in the enterprise require large teams and much coordination; so as the team grows, you see this occur. Lastly, bottom-up design does not eliminate the potential for finding design flaws that can ripple throughout the entire solution. Once discovered, these changes may cause a significant amount of work to correct. One might argue that if your team is using bottom-up design, then it would be in a better position to identify and correct large scale design flaws, but nevertheless, this approach does not make your project immune to large scale refactoring efforts caused by design issues.

Approach to Architectural Design
- What is the right choice?
  - They both are

- It is up to you as the architect to decide which approach is best for your particular project, team and organization
- Guidance:
    - Top-down will serve you well in the enterprise
    - Much of your management will be familiar with top-down
    - Top-down is useful when high-level estimates are required
    - Top-down is often a better fit with big projects and large teams
    - Bottom-up is extremely effective on small projects with just a handful of developers

So what is the right choice? I tipped my hat a bit already so I'm sure you won't be surprised when I say they really both are. Each approach has its merits and it's up to you as the architect to decide which is best for your particular project, team, and organization. So with that said, I will offer some guidance. The top-down approach will serve you well in the enterprise because it's a more structured approach that can be used for forecasting and planning. It's the approach that much of your organization's management will be familiar with and comfortable with. While bottom-up has been embraced by much of the development community, it's still not always embraced at the higher levels of many organizations. I'm not saying you shouldn't use bottom-up in the enterprise, I'm saying that when you choose to use it be prepared to explain its merits. There are still many development managers in large organizations that have not yet embraced it. Additionally, as an architect, you will be asked to provide high-level estimates to the business to determine project feasibility and resourcing needs. When this is the case, the top-down approach is useful to help understand the entirety of the project. Generally I find for big projects with large teams, top-down is often a better fit. On small projects with just a handful of developers, bottom-up is extremely effective. Projects utilizing bottom-up design produce results much faster, which can be quite motivating to both your customers and the development team. When this approach is used, it will become imperative to implement unit testing and continuous integration to maintain quality and identify emergent issues.

Approach to Architectural Design
- Personal recommendation and insights
  - I like using both approaches
  - Benefits of each approach can be realized when using the right mix
  - Great number of benefits come with embracing a top-down at inception
  - Typically will spend some time creating a high-level architecture

- Provides just enough structure
- Can be used by the development team to create more detailed designs or to help organize sprints
- Hybrid approach introduces some structure to the project at the inception but allows for evolutionary design to occur

Personally, I like using both approaches on my projects and suspect many of my peers do as well. I believe that the benefits of each approach can be realized when using the right mix. At the inception of the project, there are a number of great benefits that come with embracing a top-down approach. While it does require the architect to have a fairly thorough understanding of the project, it doesn't require an exhaustive requirements definition and waterfall approach to utilize it. I typically spend some time creating a high-level architecture that includes the first few levels of the solution. This provides enough structure for the remainder of the project to facilitate communication, size the project, and organize the project team. These high level designs will be used as the basis for more detailed design, but can be revised if gaps are uncovered. They are by no means set in stone. Now when I say more detailed design, I mean that they can be used by the development team to create more detailed designs or to help organize sprints when leveraging agile and bottom-up design techniques. The hybrid approach introduces some structure to the project at the inception, but allows for evolutionary design to occur within the high-level structures that I've defined. This approach provides structure, but allows many design decisions to be deferred until the team is much further along in the project and has a better understanding of the problem domain. Now that we've covered the two fundamental approaches to design, I'd like to spend some time discussing the design process.

Architectural Design Process

Architectural Design Process
- One technique to design your solution
- Top-down functional decomposition
- End result will be a high-level architecture
- High-level architecture used to create more detailed design
- High-level architecture could be used by an agile team practicing emergent architecture
- Introduction to design process

Before we walk through the architectural design process, I just want to let you know that this is but one technique to design your solution. The process I will outline is an example of a top-down functional decomposition where the end result will be a high-level architecture. This high-level architecture would be used by either an application architect or development team to create a more detailed design that addresses implementation-specific concerns. When using this approach, the high-level architecture could be used by an agile team

131

practicing emergent architecture; emergent architecture within the bounds of the high-level architecture that is. If you are new to architecture, this section will give you a good introduction to the process.

Architectural Design Process

- Architectural design shares many things in common with detailed design
- Scope
    - Most difficult and costly to change
    - Architecturally significant elements
- Structures, behaviors and the relationship
- Iterative
- Layered
- Begins by defining the highest level of detail
- Make sure everyone is speaking the same language
- Define a common set of terms
    - Keep them simple and be consistent

Architectural design shares many things in common with detailed design; however, there is one important difference: Scope. The scope of the architectural design are the elements of the solution that are most difficult and costly to change. These are traditionally referred to as architecturally significant elements. The architectural design defines the structures, behaviors, and the relationships between the elements that make up a solution. Design is Iterative, Layered, and Begins by defining the highest level of detail, then progressing on to the next, providing greater and greater detail at each level. The process begins by making sure everyone is speaking the same language and defining a common set of terms for your team is essential. Common terms should be defined so that the entire team understands context when talking about the elements that make up the solution. Keep them simple and consistent. The terms we'll be using in this example are System, Subsystem, Module, and Component.

Architectural Design Process

- System
    - Highest level of detail
    - Defines the entire scope of the project
    - Made up of one or many subsystems
- Subsystem
    - Logical separations of responsibility
    - Groupings of related elements
    - Sometimes a standalone application
- Module
    - Logical separations of responsibility
    - High-level groupings of other modules or components
    - Responsibilities are easily understood by the entire team
- Components
    - Execution units in our solution
    - Designed to be pluggable
    - Defined by their interfaces and behaviors

A System is the highest level of detail and it defines the entire scope of the project. A

System is made up of one or many Subsystems. Subsystems are logical separations of responsibility within the system boundary. Subsystems are groupings of related elements that comprise the entirety of your solution. A Subsystem can sometimes be a standalone application that is part of your solution. A few examples would be a web application, a console application, service, batch process workflow or even an orchestration tool. Modules are also logical separations of responsibility; however, they're comprised of high-level groupings of other modules or components whose responsibilities are easily understood by the entire team. Components are the execution units in our solution. They are independently deployable software elements. Much like their electrical counterparts, components are often designed to be pluggable and are defined by their interfaces and behaviors.

Architectural Design Process

- Each terms defines an element and a hierarchy
- Systems will include one or many subsystems
- Subsystems will include one or many modules
- Use of these exact terms is not important
- Defining YOUR terms is what's important
- Don't get lost in the details
- Use a horizontal approach

Each of these terms defines an element and a hierarchy that we used in your design. Systems will include one or many subsystems, which will include one ore many modules and so on. The use of these exact terms is not important. What is important is to make sure everyone on your team adopts and understands your terms for the elements of your design. It's important not to get lost in the details, so a horizontal approach, where each level of the solution is defined before moving on to the next, is recommended. This allows an architect to design complete levels of a solution before moving on to the next. I'm using the term level here when referring to the decomposition process instead of layers. I'm doing this intentionally so that there's no confusion when we discuss layers and tiers later.

Architectural Design Process

- **Design Considerations**
  - What are the goals & objectives of your architecture?
  - What style of application will best meet your needs?
  - What are the architectural significant requirements that should be considered?
  - How does this design account for them?
  - What are the important system, run-time, design and user quality attributes of the solution?
  - How are these addresses in the architecture?
  - Do any of these attributes have competing goals?
  - Which attributes are more important and what are the

tradeoffs that should be considered?

- What are the technical concerns of the solution?
- Have you accounted for cross cutting concerns?
- Will you utilize existing frameworks or create some as part of your project?
- What patterns should be considered?
- Have you considered technology, team, deployment and time constraints?
- Are there alternative architectures that should be considered?

- All of these are important considerations that will impact and guide your design choices

There are a number of key areas of concern that should be considered throughout the design process. Some important questions you should be asking yourself are, "What are the goals and objectives of your architecture? " And of your organization? "What style of application will best meet your needs? " Mobile, web, service oriented? "What are the architecturally significant requirements that should be considered? " And "How does this design account for them? " "What are the important system, run-time, design, and user quality attributes of the solution" and how are these addressed in your architecture? "Do any of these attributes have competing goals? " "Which attributes are more important and what are the tradeoffs that should be considered? "

What are the technical concerns of the solution? Have you accounted for cross cutting concerns? Will you utilize existing frameworks or create some as part of your project? What patterns should be considered? Have you considered technology, team, deployment and time constraints? All impact your design choices. Are there alternate architectures that should be considered? These should include off-the-shelf solutions that might be more cost effective or better meet your time constraints. All of these are important considerations that will impact and guide your design choices. Remember, this is an iterative approach so we don't have to tackle everything at once. With these considerations at hand and the understanding that design is iterative, let's now discuss how to tackle the design process. One approach is to design the solution and horizontal levels beginning with your solutions role in the organization's ecosystem. This is the approach we'll discuss for the remainder of this section.

Architectural Design Process

- Step 1: Start with the big picture & know your boundaries
  - Where does your solution fit into your organization's ecosystem?
  - Will this solution interoperate with other systems within your organization?
  - Will this solution be a standalone application?
  - Will other applications use the database you are creating?

- Will your application provide or consume any services?
- Will this application access database that are not part of your solution?
- Determine the solution's responsibilities
- Determine how it will function as a part of your organizations ecosystem
- Take note of all systems that your solution will interact with and how they will communicate
- Boundaries create context

The first level of the architectural design defines your application boundaries and interoperation points with other applications, both internal and external to your organization. Begin by understanding where your solution fits into your organization's ecosystem. A few questions you might ask are, Will the solution interoperate with other systems within your organization? Or will it be a standalone application that provides one simple function? Another question might be, Will other applications use the database you're creating? Will your application provide or consume any services? And lastly, Will this application access databases that are part of your solution? The first step is to understand questions like these to determine what the solution's responsibilities are and how it will function as part of your organization's ecosystem. Take note of all the systems that your solution will interact with and how it will communicate with them. Boundaries are an important consideration when designing a solution. Boundaries create context so use them as part of the design process to focus your attention to one particular problem at a time. In this case, we're at the top level so boundaries here are within the context of the entire solution. Anything inside these boundaries is part of that solution.

Architectural Design Process

- Step 2: Define your subsystems
  - Identify subsystems that comprise the solution
  - Subsystems are logical separations of responsibility within the system boundary
  - Subsystems are groupings of related elements that comprise the entirety of your solution
  - Subsystems may be partitioned by application type
  - If subsystems interact with each other, how and what they communicate, must be considered
  - Inventory of all subsystems, an understanding of their responsibilities and how they interact with each other

The next step is to identify subsystems that comprise the solution. Remember, subsystems are simply logical separations of responsibility within the system boundary. Subsystems are groupings of related elements that comprise the entirety of your solution. If your solution contains many architecture types like web, services, and mobile, then it's likely that the subsystems will be partitioned by application type. If subsystems interact with each other, how and what they communicate must be considered. At the end of this step you should have an inventory of all subsystems, an understanding of their responsibilities, and how they interact with each other. If any of these subsystems interact with external systems, then this interoperation should be identified. It's important to note that in some cases a solution may only have one subsystem. When this is the case, then this step is unnecessary. Remember, we've not yet begun documenting; we're just taking inventory of all the high level subsystems that make up the solution. This process is often performed on a white board, with notecards, or on paper. Regardless of your choice of medium, it's the process we're focusing on here and not the medium or the notation utilized. It is, however, important to note that one of the goals of the design process is to create a sketch of the architectural design that will be used as the basis for your documentation.

Architectural Design Process
- Step 3: Define your modules
  - Identify all modules that make up each subsystem
  - Subsystems contain one or many modules
  - Modules are dedicated to a single logical area of responsibility
  - Modules are high-level groupings of other modules
  - Modules will be defined for every subsystem proceeding

horizontally from one subsystem to the next
- Interoperation between modules is important

Once all your subsystems are defined, the next step is to identify all the modules that make up each subsystem. Subsystems contain one or many modules, each dedicated to a single logical area of responsibility. Modules are essentially high-level groupings of other modules or components whose responsibilities are easily understood by the entire team, including your non-technical team members. Modules will be defined for every subsystem proceeding horizontally from one subsystem to the next until all modules for all subsystems are defined. As with subsystems, interoperation between modules is important; however, at this level we must stay within the boundaries of the subsystem.

Architectural Design Process
- Solution decomposed into 3 levels
  - System
  - Subsystems
  - Modules
- High-level architecture or HLA
  - System boundaries
  - External interoperation points
  - Subsystems
  - Subsystem types
  - Subsystem interoperation points
  - Modules
  - Validates, constrains and provides structure
  - Used as the basis for team organization

- Serves as an architectural constraint for more detailed design

At this point, our solution has been decomposed into 3 levels: System, Subsystem, and Modules. These three levels are often referred to as a high-level architecture or HLA. The HLA defines system boundaries, external interoperation points, subsystems, subsystem types, subsystem interoperation points, modules, and their responsibilities. This is the last level of decomposition that is targeted to both non-technical and technical team members. The HLA will be used to validate, constrain, and provide structure to the remaining design steps. One of the benefits of the HLA is that it can be used as a basis for team organization. Teams can be assigned to entire subsystems or modules quite easily because each focuses on a single functional responsibility that can be developed independent of the other subsystems or modules. Depending on the size of your project and your team's experience, it may be desirable to have the development team complete the next few decomposition steps. If your development teams are using the agile methodology and embrace emergent architecture, then this document would serve as an architectural constraint that your development team would work within.

Architectural Design Process
- Step 4: Define your components
  - Define the components that make up or map to each module

- Independently deployable software elements
- Designed to be pluggable
- Defined by their interfaces and behaviors
- Responsible for a single function
- Provide replaceable, independent and encapsulated elements
- Should be loosely coupled
- Provide much flexibility in deployment
- Lower levels of design should be performed by development team
- Level of decomposition required is up to the architect

The next step in the design process is to define the components that make up or map to each of your modules. Components can be thought of as independently deployable software elements. Software components are much like their electrical counterparts, they're designed to be pluggable and are defined by their interfaces and behaviors. They're responsible for a single function and provide replaceable, independent, and encapsulated elements of your architecture. Components should be loosely coupled so that they can be easily replaced by using techniques like dependency injection. Components additionally provide much flexibility in deployment as they can be moved between tiers. We'll discuss tiers in the next section. Component design will be the lowest level of decomposition that I would suggest be performed as part of your architectural design. It's my belief that lower levels of design, like class design, are within the purview of the development team and not the architect. With that said, there are no hard and fast rules that dictate where architecture design ends and where more detailed design begins. The level of decomposition required is up to the architect and that is you. One general exception I make to my rule of not creating class designs is when my development team is made up of primarily junior developers. When this is the case, I look at it as a mentoring and training opportunity and take the time to create lower level designs that I'll present to the team. These designs aren't intended to constrain their creativity, but to help them get better at their craft.

Architectural Design Process

- When to use prototypes
    - Prototypes help to reduce risk by proving or validate design concepts
    - Prototyping is often a necessary tool for the more risky and lesser understood parts of the solution
    - Prototypes are often created by the architect
    - May be assigned to individuals on the development team if desired
    - Prototypes prove concepts to be used as examples during construction
    - Providing time constraints will help to keep the task focused

During design, you'll often identify parts of the solution that need further investigation. This can occur with new technologies and when solving complex domain problems. When this happens, prototypes may be leveraged. Prototypes help to reduce risk by proving or validating design concepts at the early stages of the project. Prototyping is often a necessary tool for the more risky and lesser understood parts of the solution. Prototypes are often created by the architect, but they may be assigned to individuals on the development team if desired. When assigned to developers, make sure you define the goals of the prototype and provide time constraints. Prototypes during design are to prove concepts or to be used as examples during construction. Providing time constraints will help to keep the task focused on the goals you set forth.

Architectural Design Process
- Architectural patterns
  - Architectural patterns help to solve recurring and well understood architectural problems
  - Architectural patterns deal with the structure and organization of the entire system or subsystem
  - Design patterns solve well understood problems encountered during construction
- Benefits of architectural patterns
  - Solve recurring problems
  - Provide a common language or short hand

- Promote high level discussions
- Simplify the design process

Patterns are another tool that you should have in your toolbox. Architectural patterns help to solve recurring and well understood architectural problems. Architectural patterns deal with the structure and organization of the entire system or subsystem. One example of an architectural pattern is the model view controller pattern. This pattern describes how a system's user interface should be structured for a web-based application. This is an architectural decision because it solves a problem at the system level. This is quite different from design patterns, which deal with a much narrower scope of problems. Design patterns solve well understood problems encountered during construction. Some examples of design patterns are singleton and factory method patterns. These patterns look to solve specific problems developers might encounter during construction and while they may be implemented in any number of places within a system, they do not apply to the solution in its entirety. Architectural patterns provide a number of benefits to the architect. As I just mentioned, they solve recurring problems, but additionally they provide a common language or shorthand that is well understood and can be used to discuss design concepts without the need for detailed explanations related to implementation. This shorthand helps to promote high-level discussions within the team during design, allowing you and your team to weigh alternatives before deciding on a particular path. This helps to simplify the design process in later discussions when communicating the architecture to your team.

Architectural Design Process

- Architectural patterns
    - May be more than one architectural pattern utilized in your solution
    - Should be used as a starting point
    - Don't be afraid to modify to solve your particular problem
    - Patterns are descriptions of solutions, not implementations
    - Don't get too hung up on applying patterns
    - Intended to provide guidance when encountering common problems
    - Patterns must be adapted to address YOUR particular problem domain

A few important notes about architectural patterns: There are often many parts to any given solution, and as such, there may be many patterns applied. This typically happens at the subsystem level, so understand that there may be more than one architectural pattern utilized in your solution. Architectural patterns should be used as a starting point so don't be afraid to modify them as needed to solve your particular problem. Remember, patterns are descriptions of solutions, not implementations. Don't get too hung up on applying patterns to every aspect of your architecture either. Patterns are great tools. Sometimes they fit and can be a tremendous asset, but sometimes they're just too complex for the needs of your solutions, so only use them when they apply and they're practical. They're intended to provide guidance when encountering common problems, but they often must be adapted to address your particular problem domain.

Architectural Design Process

- What is the right solution?
    - No single right solution to every problem
    - Almost infinite number of ways to solve any particular problem
    - Don't get too hung up on making sure your ideas are always the best
    - Primary goal: find the best solution
    - Best meets the functional, non-functional and business goals
    - Sometimes we need to check our egos at the door

The last thing I want to touch on before we move on may seem obvious, but I feel it needs to be mentioned. As architects, we must always remember that there's no single right solution to every problem. Now I realize everyone taking this book understands this, but we often lose sight of the fact when working with a team and especially during the design process. So let me remind you once again; there are an almost infinite number of ways to solve any particular problem, so don't get too hung up on making sure your ideas are always the best. The primary goal of the design process is to find the best solution. This is the solution that best meets the functional, non-functional, and business goals of the problem. Sometimes we must check our egos at the door if we want to truly find that best solution.

Communicating the Solution

Communicating the Solution
- Communicating the design to your stakeholders
- Design and documentation are two distinct processes
- Design identifies all the structures that make up the solution
- Documentation communicates design structures
- Artifacts are representations of the architecture
- Created to communicate information to a particular audience
- No right or wrong number of artifacts
- Size and makeup of your team determines the number and detail
- On small teams a high level architecture document may be sufficient
- When the team grows so do the benefits of documentation

Now that I've walked you through the design process, I'd like to focus on communicating that design to your stakeholders, both technical and non-technical. I've separated design and documentation intentionally to highlight the point that these are actually two distinct processes, both with different goals. One of the main goals of the design process was to identify all the structures that make up the solution. Now that we've identified these structures, we must now effectively communicate these structures to our audience and remember our audience is not just developers. Architectural artifacts are representations of the architecture and are created to communicate information to a particular audience. Some of these artifacts will target business stakeholders, some will target technical, and some will target both. There's no right or wrong number of artifacts required to communicate your solution. This is entirely dependent on what you're attempting to communicate and to whom. The size and makeup of your team will help to determine the number of artifacts and the detail needed. On small teams, creating lots of design documents will not provide as much value as on a large team. There are economies of scale that occur when a team grows past the 5-10 person mark that contribute to the overall benefit of creating these design artifacts. When your teams are small, the entire development team can participate in the design process, working side by side with the architect. A simple high level architecture document may be sufficient after the entire team has participated in the design. When the team grows past the 5-10 person mark, the time needed for an architect to communicate design changes and educate team members increases, making it much less effective as on a small team.

Communicating the Solution

- The more complex the design, the more the need to create an artifact

- Don't forget about your non-technical stakeholders
- Small teams balloon quickly
- Time spent documenting pales in comparison to the time spent
  - Communicating the design
  - Educating new team members
  - Justifying and explaining design decisions
- Artifacts can do much of this for you
- Artifacts help you scale
- Blueprint upon which to construct the solution
- Why decisions were made
- What should be considered in the future
- Value provided is much greater than cost
- You will never be able to scale as well as your artifacts

The complexity of the design also contributes to the decision. The more complex the design, the more the need to create an artifact that explains the solution. When you have a simple solution or one that utilizes well understood architectural patterns, then the need to create artifacts describing that solution decreases. It's equally important to consider non-technical stakeholders as it is to consider technical stakeholders. Your non-technical team is most likely made up of business stakeholders, project managers, business analysts, quality assurance testers, managers, directors, the list goes on and on. Your small team balloons very quickly once you start to consider the number of people that will use these artifacts. Once this is considered, the time spent creating these documents often pales in comparison to the time you'll need to spend communicating the design, educating the new team members, justifying and explaining design decisions without them. Artifacts can do much of this for you. They'll help you scale as your team grows. Additionally, it's also important to consider that you're not only creating a blueprint upon which to construct the solution, but a document that will communicate to future stakeholders why decisions were made, as well as what should be considered in the future. As your team grows, it should become very apparent that the value provided by these documents is much greater than the cost in time and effort that it will take to create them. Remember, you'll never be able to scale as well as your artifacts will.

Communicating the Solution

- Three main objectives for creating architectural artifacts
- Objective 1: Facilitate communication between stakeholders
  - Communicate what is being built
  - How functional and quality related requirements are being achieved
  - Communicate system constraints
  - Blueprint serves as the interface
  - Define the structures
  - Define the terms upon which the team will communicate
  - Communicate meaningfully within and between teams

- Objective 2: Basis for detailed design and construction efforts
  - Provide a foundation
  - Provide guidance, structure and constraints
- Objective 3: Educate the team, both business and technical
  - Educate both technical and non-technical stakeholders
  - Facilitate discussions
  - Provide background
  - Explain choices
  - Document decisions
  - Provide context and abstraction
  - Provide a basis for educating

There are three main objectives for creating architectural artifacts. The first is to produce architectural artifacts that will communicate what is being built to your non-technical stakeholders and how functionality and quality-related requirements are being achieved. At the same time, it's also important to communicate system constraints to your technical stakeholders that must be abided when implementing the solution. These blueprints additionally serve as the interface between the non-technical and technical stakeholders. They define the structures from the top-down and from the bottom-up. These artifacts will be used to define the terms upon which the team will communicate while the project is active into document decisions after the project has been completed. Creating a common lexicon that can be utilized by both your non-technical and technical stakeholders is of critical importance to the success of your project. It will allow all your stakeholders to communicate meaningfully within and between teams. The second objective is to provide the foundation upon which non-architectural, more detailed designs, and construction will be built. Architectural artifacts should provide guidance, structure, and constraints, which help direct the development team toward the solution that meets the needs of the business. The third objective is to educate both technical and non-technical stakeholders. Architectural artifacts are used to facilitate discussions, provide background, explain choices, and document decisions that occur throughout the life of the project. As solutions become more and more complex, these artifacts are needed by both technical and non-technical stakeholders. They help to provide context and abstraction, simplifying the complexity of the solution. They provide a basis for education and ramping up team members as they are added to the project.

Communicating the Solution

- How do we know we are meeting these objectives?
    - Ask yourself two questions
    - Does this document provide value?
    - Does this level of detail communicate enough?
    - Second question tells us when to stop
    - Is there enough detail for our business users to understand how we are meeting their needs?

- Is there enough detail for our development team to build a solution?
- When both of these questions are answered then you have provided enough detail

So how do we know we're meeting these objectives with our artifacts? One test is to ask yourself two simple questions every time you create an architectural artifact. The first question is, Does this document provide value in at least one of the areas I identified as objectives? The second is, Does this level of detail communicate enough to the intended audience or will I need to provide another level of detail to meet these goals? The second question is crucial because it tells us when to stop. Remember, we're not attempting to communicate every detail of the system. Our goal is to define just enough to communicate what we're building to a particular audience. Is there enough detail for our business users to understand how we're meeting their needs? Is there enough detail for our development team to build a solution? When both of these questions are answered, then you have provided enough detail.

Communicating the Solution
- Documentation Standards
  - Focus on diagrams
  - Diagrams are more effective for communicating complex concepts
  - 3 Categories: Formal, Informal and Hybrid

Now that we have an understanding of the objectives when creating architectural artifacts, let's spend some time discussing types and styles. I'm going to focus on diagrams primarily because this is where we get the most value from abstraction. There is much value from writing prose, but diagrams are a much more effective tool for communicating complex concepts. When speaking specifically about architectural diagrams, we can split this into 3 categories: Communicating the Solution

- Formal
    - Unified Modeling Language or UML
    - Industry standard language for modeling
    - 14 types of diagrams
    - Two categories
        - Structural
        - Behavioral
    - Structural diagrams define the structures that makeup the application
    - Behavioral diagrams represent the behavior and functionality
    - Interaction diagrams represent the control flow between components
    - Adoption is not widespread
    - Usage is inconsistent
    - Very good at low level documentation
    - Not as straightforward for higher levels

The first is a Formal notation most often represented by Unified Modeling Language or UML. UML is the industry standard language for modeling. The 2. 2 standard is comprised of 14 types of diagrams that are separated into two categories: Structural and Behavioral. As the category name suggests, Structural diagrams are used to define the structures that make up the application. And Behavioral diagrams represent the behavior and functionality of the systems components. There are additionally a subset of diagrams within the Behavioral category, Interaction diagrams, that represent the control flow between components. Even though UML is the industry standard, its adoption has not been widespread. Many developers don't know or understand the notation, so its usage has been inconsistent. UML is very good at low level documentation like class, sequence, activity, diagrams, but at the higher levels like architectural diagrams, it's not as straightforward. I personally believe that it's the UML's perceived complexity and rigidity that are stopping widespread adoption. We're beginning to see IDEs like Visual Studio incorporate modeling tools. These efforts have the potential to inject UML into standard development processes and may help with adoption so long as the productivity benefits outweigh the cost and time and effort to the development team. Communicating the Solution

- Informal
  - Box and line diagrams
  - Most common type of diagram
  - Barrier of entry is low
  - No constraints
  - Easily expressed
  - No rules to break
  - Adoption is easy and widespread

- Ambiguous, imprecise and disorganized

Informal notation consists primarily of box and line diagrams that represent structure, behavior, and relationships between elements. This is probably the most common type of diagram because the barrier of entry is extremely low. Box and line diagrams have no constraints on the author so they're easily expressed on white boards and on diagramming tools. There are no rules to break so adoption is easy and widespread. However, with no rules, box and line diagrams are often ambiguous, imprecise, and disorganized.

Communicating the Solution

- Hybrid
  - Non-standard UML diagrams in conjunction with box and line drawings
  - Martin Fowler -3 modes of UML diagrams
    - Sketch
    - Blueprints
    - Programming language
  - Sketch is most common
  - Sketch doesn't necessarily conform to all the rules of UML
  - Selectively communicating concepts and ideas
  - Non-standard usage of UML is hybrid approach
  - Natural progression from sketches to blueprints
  - Blueprints are the architectural diagrams that are the focus of this section

158

The Hybrid approach is the use of non-standard UML diagrams in conjunction with box and line drawings. In his book UML Distilled 3rd Edition, Martin Fowler discusses how UML is evolving into 3 modes or types of UML diagrams: Sketch, Blueprints, and Programming language, the most common of which is Sketch. The sketch doesn't necessarily conform to all the rules of UML; its focus is on selectively communicating concepts and ideas rather than complete specifications. This non-standard usage of UML is what I would describe as a hybrid approach and fits nicely into an iterative approach to architectural design. Fowler goes on to describe blueprints as a more formal approach to UML. There's a natural progression from sketches that are created during the design process in the blueprints. Blueprints are in essence the architectural diagrams that are the focus of this section.

Communicating the Solution
- Personal recommendations
  - Use hybrid approach
  - Use UML selectively
  - Hybrid approach provides best of both worlds
  - Martin Fowlers "UML distilled" is a good starting point

Personally, I have adopted the hybrid approach and suspect many of my peers have done as well. Depending on the size and complexity of the project, UML can sometimes be too heavy for our needs so I use it selectively. UML provides a standard and foundation that can be leveraged and built upon. The adoption of a hybrid approach allows you the best of both worlds; it allows you to leverage the UML where it's practical and where there's standard diagrams that fit your needs. Like everything else, the best way to learn something is just to start using it. Martin Fowler's "UML distilled" is a short read and will give you enough information to get started.

What are Views?

What are views?
- A window into the architecture
- Single viewpoint targeted to a particular audience
- No single view
- No set number and types of views
- The architecture is comprised of all the views
- Several well-known approaches rely on of views

So now that we have an understanding of the objectives and types of documentation, let's discuss how we're going to meet our objectives using the types of documentation notation we discussed. For this we must introduce the concept of views. A view can be thought of as a window into the architecture. Each window supplies only a single viewpoint that is targeted to a particular audience and addresses a specific set of concerns. There's no single view that represents the entire architecture and there are no set number of types of views that are required to communicate in architecture.

The architecture is comprised of all the views
necessary to effectively communicate how
the solution will be structured to meet the
quality attributes of the solution. There are
several well-known approaches to
architectural documentation that rely on the
concept of views as a fundamental concept.
One of the more well-known is the 4+1
architectural view.

4+1 architectural view model

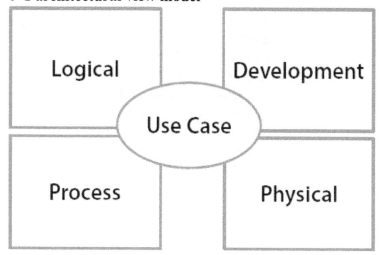

- 5 views
- Each address a separate set of
  concerns and audience

In this approach, the architecture is
represented by 5 views, each addressing a
separate set of concerns and audience.

Use Case

- Ties all of the other views together
- User requirements
- System functionality
- Internal and external actors
- Represented using use UML case
  diagrams

The scenario, or use case view, is central and
it ties all the other views together. This

161

viewpoint addresses user requirements, system functionality, and both internal and external factors of the system. This viewpoint is often represented using the UML case diagram.

Logical

- End user functionality viewpoint
- Structures of the architecture that implement functional requirements
- Classes and their relationships
- Represented using UML class diagrams

The Logical view in the top left quadrant represents the end user functionality viewpoint. This viewpoint addresses the structures of the architecture that implement the functional requirements, namely classes, and their relationships. This viewpoint is often represented using UML class diagrams.

Process

- Run-time viewpoint
- Performance
- Reliability
- Scalability
- Interaction and communication
- Represented using UML activity diagrams

The Process view on the bottom left represents a run-time viewpoint. This viewpoint addresses Performance, Reliability, Scalability, and how the elements will interact and communicate with each other at run-time. This viewpoint is often represented using UML activity diagrams.

Development

- Structure & organizational viewpoint
- Modules are organized

- Module interaction
- Represented with a UML package and component diagram

The Development view in the top right quadrant represents a structure and organizational viewpoint. This viewpoint addresses how modules are organized and how they interact. This viewpoint is often represented with a UML package and component diagram.

Physical
- Infrastructure viewpoint
- Deployment
- Communications between physical tiers
- Represented with a UML deployment diagram

The Physical view or Deployment view in the bottom right quadrant represents the infrastructure viewpoint. This viewpoint addresses where the solution will be deployed and the communications between these physical tiers. This viewpoint is often represented with a UML deployment diagram.

- Each view targets a specific set of stakeholders and concerns
- 5 view categories represent the whole of the architecture

This approach makes a lot of sense when you consider that each view targets a specific set of stakeholders and concerns. The 5 view categories represent the whole of the architecture and organizes it very intuitively.

Views & Beyond

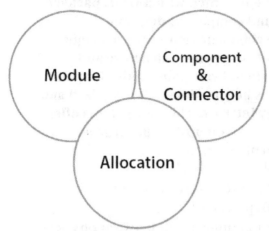

- **Documenting Software Architectures: Views and Beyond (2nd Edition): Paul Clements, Felix Bachmann, Len Bass, David Garlan, James Ivers, Reed Little, Paulo Merson, Robert Nord, Judith Stafford**
- **3 view categories**
- **Each represent a distinct set of styles**

Another view-based approach can be found in the text, Documenting Software Architectures: Views and Beyond (2nd Edition). The authors of this text took the 4+1 approach and built on it. In the Views and Beyond approach, the authors identify 3 view categories, each representing a distinct set of styles that represent a viewpoint of the architecture. These view categories are the Module, Component and Connector, and Allocation views.

Views & Beyond

- **Multiple views styles**
- **Enumerate, organize and describe common view styles**
- **Prescribe notation used for each style**

- View styles are often combined

Each view category contains multiple view styles. The text seeks to enumerate, organize, and describe common view styles while prescribing the notation that should be used when selecting a particular style. The text goes on to explain that view styles are often combined when being applied to a diagram.

Views & Beyond

- Provide a style guide that describes notation
- Concise, understood and consistent
- UML only solves part of the problem
- Still a need to use informal and hybrid notation

One of the more notable points in the text, at least from my perspective anyway, is that the authors' desire is to provide a guide or standard to our industry that describes notation so that architectural documentation is concise, understood, and consistent. The authors recognize that even though we have a notation standard in UML, it only solves part of the problem. There's still a need to use informal and hybrid notation approaches when UML just doesn't fit the bill.

Views & Beyond

- No single industry standard approach to architectural documentation
- Offer their text as a guide
- Other valid approaches
- Documentation must be standardized

The underlying message is that there's not currently a single industry standard approach to architectural documentation and one is sorely needed. They offer their text as a guide, but also suggests that there are other valid approaches that can be adopted. Their goal is not to make their guide the industry standard, but to declare that documentation must be standardized, at the very least in your organization. So a style guide or standard must be utilized. If your enterprise does not have a style guide, then your choice is either to create one or to adopt one. They offer Views and Beyond as one that may be adopted.

Views & Beyond

- 3 categories of views
- Each category contains many view styles
- Each categories does not prescribe number of views
- Standard sets of styles that should considered
- Style guide prescribes the notation style that will be utilized

So to continue, the Views and Beyond approach identifies 3 categories of views, each category contains many view styles. Each category does not prescribe the number of views that should be created or even how to use them. What they do prescribe is that when creating certain types of views, there's a standard set of styles that should be considered. When a particular style is chosen, this style guide prescribes the notation style that should be utilized.

Views & Beyond

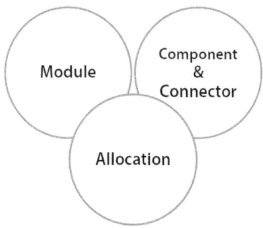

Module
- Styles
  - Decomposition
  - Uses
  - Generalization
  - Layered
  - Aspects
  - Data model
- Structural view of the architecture
- How modules are organized and how they interact
- Blueprint of the system
- Show dependencies
- Styles may be combined on any single view

So let's take a look at the three view categories. Module views are the first category and they represent the structural view of the architecture. This viewpoint addresses how modules are organized and how they interact with each other. The module views provide a blueprint of the system and are often represented by module decomposition diagrams. These views seek to show dependencies between modules and dependencies between layers within a module. Some of the main styles used when creating module views are Decomposition, Uses, Generalization, Layered, Aspects, and Data model styles. Remember, these styles may be combined on any single view.

Component& Connector

- Styles
    - Data flow
    - Call-return
    - Event-based
    - Repository
- Behavioral view of the architecture
- How the elements of the system work together at run-time
- How they meet performance, reliability and availability quality attributes

The Component & Connector views represent the behavioral view of the architecture. This viewpoint addresses how the elements of the system work together at run-time, how they meet performance, reliability and availability or quality requirements. Some of the main styles found when creating Component and Connector views are Data flow, Call-return, Event-based, and Repository styles.

Allocation

- Styles
    - Deployment
    - Install
    - Work assignment
- Development, deployment and execution views of the architecture
- Allocated to infrastructure and work teams

- Map elements to hardware and work teams

The Allocation views represent the development, deployment, and execution views of the architecture. This viewpoint addresses how the elements of the system are allocated to infrastructure and work teams. Views in the set map elements from your Module views and Component & Connector views to hardware and work teams. Some of the main styles when creating allocation views are Deployment, Install, and Work assignment styles.

- Views are not just made up of the architectural diagrams
- Supporting information must be presented
- Element catalog
- Variability guide
- Rationale

The text not only identifies notation styles for diagrams, but goes further to explain that views are not just made up of architectural diagrams. While this may be the primary presentation, there's supporting information that must be presented. This includes an Element catalog where each element identified in your diagram is described and whose interfaces and behaviors are notated. A Variability guide that describes the ability of the architecture to be tailored to suit the needs of the solution and a Rationale section that describes why certain design choices were made, as well as any design-related information that might be useful.

What are views?

- Many approaches to architectural documentation

169

- Mainstream approaches have adopted a view based approach
- No single document that can represent complexity
- Abstraction
- Decomposition
- Different views of the architecture
- Address a certain set of concerns
- Target a specific audience
- Not advocating the wholesale adoption of either approach
- Continue your educating with either approach
- No one size fits all approach
- Take pieces from each that best suit you, your projects and your organization

The main point I want to make here is that there are many approaches to architectural documentation and many of the mainstream approaches have adopted a view based approach. This approach acknowledges that there is no single document that can represent the complexity of most solutions. Complexity is addressed through Abstraction, Decomposition, and providing different views of the architecture. Each view is intended to address a certain set of concerns and targets a specific audience. The Views and Beyond approach goes a bit further, identifying three view categories, as well as enumerating and prescribing a set of notation styles that may be adopted. Now at this point, I want to be clear. I'm not advocating the wholesale adoption of either of these approaches. They both tend to be too heavy for many of the projects encountered in the enterprise; however, continuing your education with either of these approaches will help to provide a foundation that can be leveraged and built upon as you gain more experience as an architect. No matter what approach you adopt, it's important to keep in mind that it must be adopted for you, your project, and your organization. There's no one size fits all approach that will work for every situation. Each approach has its benefits, so approach them like a buffet and take the pieces from each that best suit you, your projects, and your organization.

Views in Practice

Views & Beyond in practice

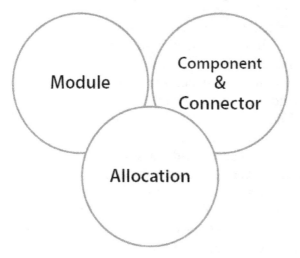

Examples

I'm going to use the Views and Beyond approach to provide a few examples in the remainder of this book. I personally find the text to be very readable and practical for most of my needs, so I've adopted many of the recommendations into my daily practice. I'm going to provide a few examples that will help get you on your way, so let's get started. The example I'd like to get started with is the Module view.

Module

- Structural view of the architecture
- How modules are organized and how they interact
- Blueprint
- Identify all the major subsystems in the solution
- Module decomposition diagram
- Boundaries of the solution, all the subsystems and their interactions

As I stated before, Module views represent the structural view of the architecture. This viewpoint addresses how modules are organized and how they interact with each other. Module views provide a blueprint of the system. These views seek to show dependencies between modules and dependencies between layers within a module. The six primary Module view styles are Decomposition, Uses, Generalization, Layered, Aspects, and Data Model styles. I typically create at least one decomposition view to identify all the major subsystems in the solution. I use this diagram to show relationships between the subsystems and to identify boundaries of the solution. My preference is to use a module decomposition diagram where packages represent subsystems with explicit uses relationships. The top-level diagram identifies the boundaries of the solution, all the subsystems, and their interactions. This is one of the most useful diagrams an architect can produce and it's a great place for us to get started.

Module View

- Module decomposition -Level 1
  - View of the entire solution from a very high level
  - Technical and non-technical team members
  - Identify all system boundaries & subsystems

The first or top-level diagram is one that provides a view of the entire solution from a very high level. This view is intended for both technical and non-technical team members and will identify the system boundaries, subsystems that comprise a solution, and interoperation points with other applications, both internal and external to the organization. The top-level diagram identifies all the subsystems that make up your solution. Subsystems are logical separations of responsibility that operate independently, sometimes they're even standalone applications. Subsystems identified at this level comprise the entirety of your solution. When subsystems interact with each other, it should be identified on this diagram. Many years ago I designed and developed web-based hotel reservation systems for a small software company. The application is still in use today and has deployed at thousands of hotel properties all over the world. The example I am going to show you is not exactly what I implemented and to be completely honest it's a bit contrived, but my goal here is to provide a few examples to help you get started.

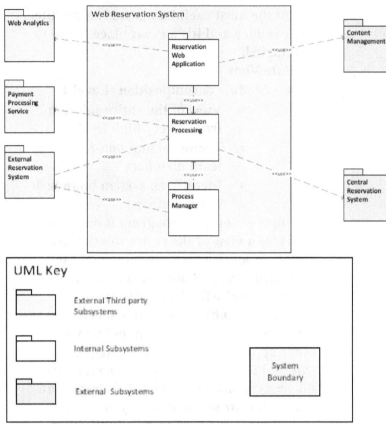

Here we see a Module-level UML diagram
for my web-based reservation system
example. This packaged diagram identifies
all the subsystems that make the solution.
The three contained within the boundary are
part of the solution. The three on the left are
third-party systems that interact with the
reservation system and the two on the right
are existing internal systems that the
reservation system will interact with. This
type of view focuses on organizing the system
into a hierarchy of modules beginning with
the system, subsystem, and module. This
view primarily targets software developers,
but when paired with Allocation views, it will
be used as the basis for resource allocation,

cost evaluation, planning, project
management, reuse, and portability. The
system, subsystem, and module hierarchy is
well understood by the technical team and
easy to understand by business stakeholders.
Decomposition diagrams progressively
describe the architecture in lower and lower
levels, so the next step in our example would
be to further define each subsystem. If we
select the reservation processing subsystem
as a starting point for the next level of
decomposition, we would have a diagram
that looked like this.

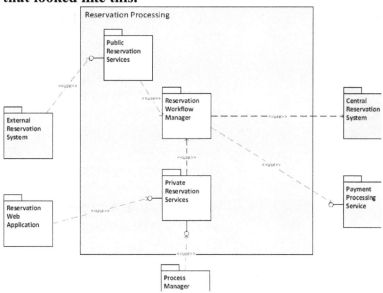

UML Key

External Third party Subsystems

Internal Module

External Module

Subsystem Boundary

Module View

- **Module decomposition -Level 2**
  - **Individual subsystems that were identified in the top level diagram**
  - **Define all modules that make up each subsystem**
  - **Subsystems contain one or many modules**
  - **Single logical area of responsibility**
  - **High-level groupings of other modules**
  - **Interoperation between modules is important**

The second level of decomposition will focus on the individual subsystems that were identified in the top-level diagram. This is where we define all modules that make up each subsystem. In this case, the reservation processing subsystem. Subsystems can contain one or many modules each dedicated to a single logical area of responsibility. Modules are essentially high-level groupings of other modules whose responsibilities are easily understood by the entire team, including non-technical team members. As with subsystems, interoperation between

176

modules is extremely important. At this level, we see that the reservation processing subsystem is composed of three modules: the Public Reservation Services, Reservation Workflow Manager, and Private Reservation Services. The diagram depicts both the internal and external interop points, as well as their relationships. I've chosen to differentiate the service modules by adding the lollipop notation to each package. Please note that I've added this to the key as well to make sure that this notation is well defined. Now that we have all modules on our Reservation Processing Subsystem defined, we can proceed one level further by further decomposing each module identified here. ModuleView

- Module decomposition -Level 3
  - No hard and fast rule that defines how many levels
  - Decompose your system to as many levels as needed
  - Decomposition is performed iteratively

I typically provide at least 3 levels of decomposition, but there's no hard and fast rule that defines how many levels you must define. A simple rule of thumb is to decompose your system to as many levels as needed to effectively communicate your architectural choices to the development team. There's also no firm rule that says you must decompose the entire system at once. Module decomposition can be done iteratively and as needed. This means that module decomposition at this level may be performed as part of your sprints if you're using an agile methodology. To continue our

example, a third level of decomposition might look like this.

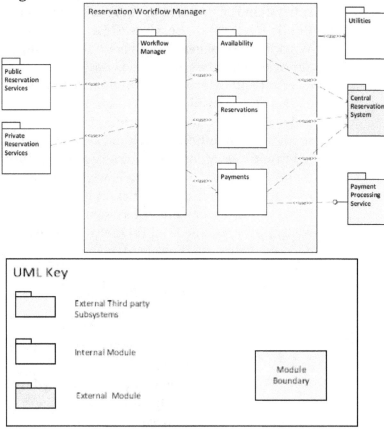

In this diagram, we depict all the submodules that make up the Reservation Workflow Module, both the internal and the external interop points, as well as their relationships. Here you can see that the Workflow Manager Module interacts with the three modules: Availability, Reservations, and Payments. The modules interact with the Central Reservation System and the Payment Processing Service, which is identified as being a third-party solution.
Module View

- Module decomposition

- Continues to lowest level of detail that provides value
- Not necessary to decompose every subsystem and every module
- Guided by practicality

This process continues to the lowest level of detail that provides a value to your project. It's not necessary to decompose every subsystem and every module. In some cases it may only be necessary to decompose just a few levels and let the development team do the rest, using either a top-down or a bottom-up approach. The detail and approach are up to you and should be guided by practicality and value, not by blindly following an approach that doesn't provide value to you and your team. It's possible to continue decomposing the solution, but at this point I think you've got the idea. The decomposition style is not the only module view style discussed in Views and Beyond. Please take note that the text offers a number of additional module styles that you should be familiar with and utilize if they provide value to your architecture. There's one additional module style that I'd like to cover in this example. It's one that you're most likely already familiar with, it's the Layered style.

Module View
- Layered
    - Separated logically by responsibility
    - Contain modules that make up each layer
    - Loosely coupled
    - Cohesive

- Manage dependencies
- Flexibility
- Maintainability
- Layers are logical
- Tiers are physical

The layered style is another extremely useful type of module view. In Layered views, layers are separated logically by responsibility and contain modules that make up each layer. Each layer has a single responsibility. Modules contained in a layer may interact only with the modules contained within it and with modules contained in the layer beneath it. Layers should be loosely coupled and modules contained within each layer should be strongly related or cohesive. Some common examples of layers are the presentation layer, business layer, data layer, and service layer that we commonly see in books and articles related to software design. Grouping modules into logical layers helps us to manage dependencies more effectively, increasing Flexibility and Maintainability of the solution. Before we proceed, we need to define the term, layers and tier, because they're often misused. Layers are the logical organization of an application, where tiers are the physical organization or implementation. The easiest way to think about this is that layers quite often run on the same machine, where tiers typically run on separate machines. Sometimes layers and tiers are the same, but it's important to note that layers are logical and tiers are physical.

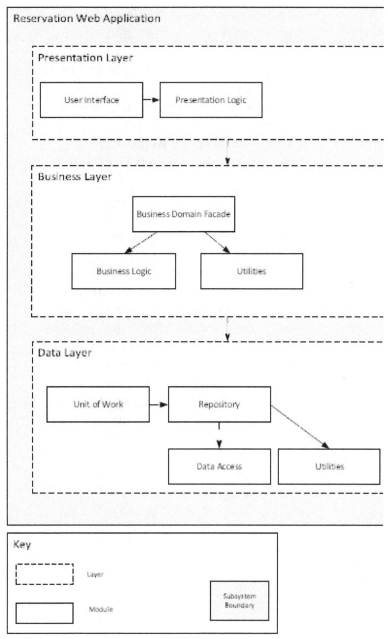

Here we see that the Reservation Web
Application is separated into three layers:
the Presentation layer, Business layer, and
Data layer. Each contains a number of

modules whose interaction is explicitly depicted. We've chosen to explicitly identify the interaction between the layers, but please note that this is not necessary as interaction downward between layers is implied simply by choosing a layered style diagram. These layers may look very familiar to you; this is because I've applied a well understood architectural pattern to our solution. Architectural patterns are well known by both architects and developers and should be leveraged when defining your layering strategy. It's the job of the architect to determine the correct layering strategy and how the layers will interact with each other. Use commonly understood architectural patterns as guidelines for your layering strategy, but don't be afraid to break the rules if they prove to be more complicated than needed. Another important layer to consider is one that isolates and identifies cross cutting concerns of an application. This is important because cross cutting concerns are dependencies for all layers within the module and often of cross modules as well. When diagramming a cross cutting concern in a layer diagram, it's often performed by adding a layer adjacent to the other layers.

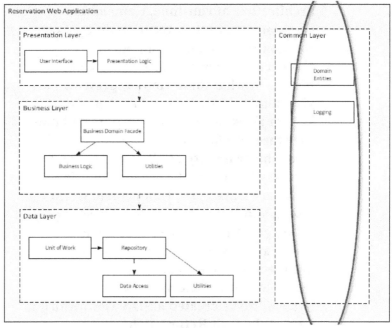

Reservation Web Application

Presentation Layer

User Interface → Presentation Logic

Business Layer

Business Domain Facade

Business Logic   Utilities

Data Layer

Unit of Work → Repository

Data Access   Utilities

Common Layer

Domain Entities

Logging

This layer is often presented vertically instead of horizontally, and because of its proximity to the other layers, its usage by all layers is implied. Sometimes arrows are used to explicitly depict its usage. In this diagram, we've added a layer that addresses the cross cutting concerns of this module. As you can see, this layer is different, it's accessible to all the others. Next, let's take a look at the Component & Connector view.

Component& Connector

- Behavioral view of the architecture at run-time
- Components are execution units
- How the elements work together at run-time
- Performance
- Reliability
- Availability

As I said before, Component & Connector views represent the behavioral view of the architecture at run-time. Remember, components are the execution units of our solution so the name Component & Connector actually paints a very clear picture of what these views represent. This viewpoint addresses how the elements of the system work together at run-time and how they meet Performance, Reliability, and Availability quality attributes. The four primary Component & Connector view styles are Data Flow, Call-return, Event based, and Repository styles. These are the broad general categories that are used to group and organize a large number of architectural style choices. To continue our example of using the Web Reservation System, we've created a SOA view, which is part of the Call-Return style.

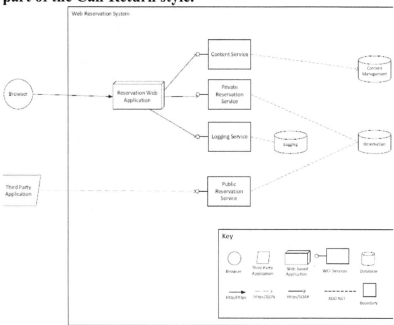

This is one that I find extremely useful because many of my projects are web and service-based. In this simple example you can see how all service providers and consumers are identified, as well as the interaction between each component. By explicitly identifying services with a distinct symbol type, you can easily understand which component is the consumer and which is the service provider. I have additionally included communication protocols and types like HTTPS, SOA, and JSON explicitly in the diagram. Including these notations helps reduce ambiguity.

Component & Connector View
- SOA
    - Identify high level service related components
    - Interactions
    - Dependencies

The intention of this diagram is to identify all high-level service-related components, their interactions, and dependencies. A view like this could be used to educate both technical and non-technical stakeholders about the significant aspects of the architecture and how they'll interact at run-time. Like module decomposition diagrams, Component & Connector views can be created for any level and for various architectural styles. Another style of Component & Connector view, which I find extremely useful, is the Tiered view.

Component & Connector View
- Tiered
    - Depicts logical groupings of execution
    - Components grouped together logically by
        - Type
        - Execution requirement

- Purpose
- Identify communication requirements between components and tiers
- Physical organization
- Deployment model

The Tiered view of an architecture depicts logical groupings of execution. Each tier contains many components grouped together logically by Type, Execution requirement or even Purpose. Tiered diagrams help to identify communication requirements between components and tiers. I use this type of diagram on most of my projects, especially where the solution is distributed across a number of hardware resources. Tiers are used to define the physical organization and deployment model for your components. This is performed by mapping the components of your application to the physical environment in which they'll run. It's important to identify what is contained in each tier and how they will communicate. It's quite common in an organization for your infrastructure choices to have already been made for you. Rarely do we implement a new system into a new infrastructure, so this exercise of defining tiers provides value and understanding of the deployment requirements, but realize you'll often not have much choice in how the solution will be deployed.

Component & Connector View

- Tiered
  - Understand deployment requirements
  - Deployment constraints are important

- Identify infrastructure challenges
- Not mapped to physical machines

These deployment constraints are extremely important for an architect to understand while designing a solution. They may impact many of his or her design decisions. The target audience for this diagram is infrastructure architects, engineers, and your deployment team. This diagram can be used to help identify where infrastructure challenges might exist for your solution. Tiers are identified by functional type, but are not mapped to physical machines. Mapping tiers to the physical machines is typically performed by an infrastructure architect as part of deployment planning.

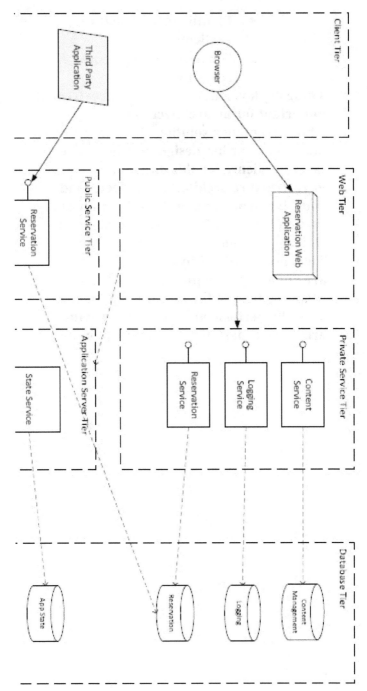

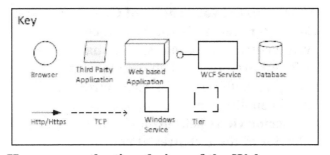

Key

Browser | Third Party Application | Web based Application | WCF Service | Database | Http/Https | TCP | Windows Service | Tier

Here we see the tiered view of the Web Reservation System. The view is quite obviously targeting the infrastructure team, depicting the six physical tiers that make up the solution. On the left side of the diagram you see the Client Tier, which represents the end users and third-party applications that interact with the solution. You can see the interaction is with the Reservation Web System via HTTP or HTTPS. This is quite common, but communicates important information to the infrastructure team on where the web and public services tier should reside. The Web Tier contains the Reservation Web Application, which communicates via HTTP to WCF services contained in the Private Services Tier, as well as services contained in the Application Server Tier. Both the Private Service Tier and the Application Server Tier communicate with the components in the Database Tier. Diagrams like this are useful in describing the types of communications that may occur across tiers. The text provides a number of additional Component & Connector view styles, each for different architectural styles.

Component & Connector View

- Guided by your architectural style
- Visualize the behavior of these choices at run-time

In most cases, your choice of Component & Connector view style will be guided by your architectural style choices. If we had made different architectural choices for our example, then our view style choices might have been different. Component & Connector views help us to visualize the behavior of these choices at run-time. Next, let's take a look at Allocation views, what they're used for, and how they're related to Module and Component & Connector views. Allocation

- Identify the mapping between software elements & non-software elements
  - System
  - Work team

The text, Views and Beyond, describes Allocation views as those views used to identify the mapping between the software elements depicted in Module and Component & Connector views and non-software elements. Non-software elements include both System related and Work team related elements. The three primary allocation styles are deployment, install, and work assignment styles. Let's first discuss Work Assignment styles and their benefits. Allocation View

- Work Assignment
  - Simple lists
  - Subsystems or modules assignments

Work Assignment views are not depicted graphically, but they do relate directly to either a Module or Component & Connector views. When I create work assignments, I always begin with the top-level module view

190

as my starting point. Work Assignment
views are Simple lists that identify
Subsystems or modules and which
development team or individuals assigned to
them.
Allocation View

Susbsytem	Module	Resource
Reservation Workflow Manager	Workflow Manager	Developer 1
	Availibility	Developer 2
	Reservations	Developer 1
	Payments	Developer 2
Reservation Services	Availibility	Developer 3
	Reservations	Developer 4
	Payments	Developer 3

- Work Assignment
  - Simple lists
  - Subsystems or modules
    assignments
  - Resource assignments may be
    performed as part of your
    sprint planning sessions

I typically create Work Assignment views
using a spreadsheet, where I identify the
subsystems in the leftmost column, then the
module, and then the resource. I often create
these lists with generic names like Developer
1 and 2 or Web Developer 1 and 2. I do this
because Work Assignment views are often
created before resources are even assigned to
a project. This helps identify the optimal
number of resources and even the type of
research needed to build a subsystem or
module. Once resources have been assigned
to a project, I then assign specific developers
that have the experience or the skill set
needed to construct the module. This may
not sound like an architect's job, but most

project managers just don't have the knowledge or experience to assign developers to particular tasks. They often look at developers as interchangeable, where any developer can perform any task in the same amount of time. Everyone taking this book understands that not all developers are created equal. Some are better suited to certain tasks. It's important to assign tasks to individuals that can best accomplish them. If you're using an agile methodology, then resource-specific assignments may be performed as part of your sprint planning sessions. The last type of Allocation view I'd like to discuss is the Deployment view.

Allocation View

- **Deployment**
    - **Map components to physical machines**
    - **Performance**
    - **Availability**
    - **Reliability**
    - **Security**
    - **Use generic like Server A and B**

The Deployment view is used to map components from your Component & Connector views directly to physical machines. It's also used to illustrate how Performance, Availability, Reliability, and Security quality attributes are met by the solution. It's been my experience that this view is often the responsibility of infrastructure architects that have been assigned to your team; however, if your organization does not have infrastructure architects, then the job may fall to you. I often create the first version of these views, but leave the server names generic like Server A and B. I then present this view of the infrastructure team to assign actual machine names. This works well because at design time we often don't know the physical or virtual machine where the solution will be deployed. Here's an example of a fairly simple Deployment diagram.

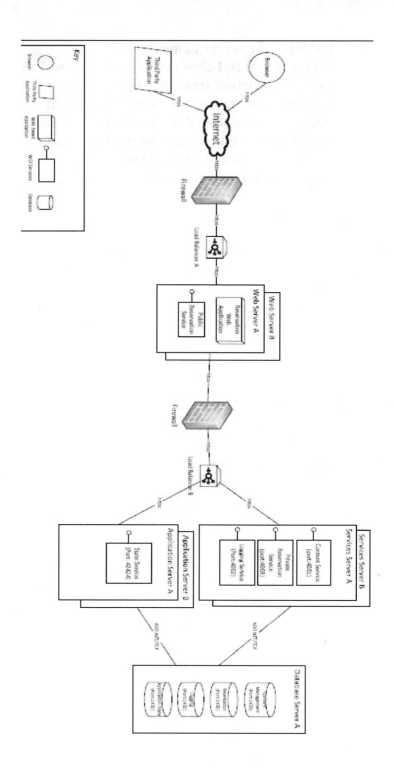

This diagram depicts many of the components that were identified on our Component & Connector diagrams; however, we've added a few additional elements, namely firewalls, load balancers, and servers. Reading left to right, this diagram looks very similar to our tiered diagram, with the clients here on the left, followed by the web presentation tier in the middle, and the two service tiers and database tiers on the right. Additionally, there are machine names or machine name placeholders included to be assigned later. Because this is a service-oriented architecture, I've explicitly identified each components port on the diagram. HTTP and HTTPS use standard ports 80 and 443, so explicitly naming them doesn't provide any value to the diagram. This diagram also depicts that the services communicate directly with the database server, specifically using port 1433. Identifying communication type and port is important because both are often restricted via firewall rules. Unless these requirements are identified to the infrastructure team, it's likely communication between components will be restricted when you deployed your production environment. Including communication protocols and ports, firewall, and load balancing information on your Deployment view speaks directly to the performance, availability, reliability, and security quality attributes of the solution. The text includes a few more Allocation views that I encourage you to review. Remember, there's no one size fits all to choosing which views you should include in your project. It's your job to educate yourself on what is available and then to decide what provides value to your project and your organization.

Views & Beyond

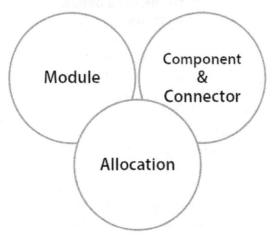

- **Diagram is the primary presentation**
- **Element catalog**
- **Variability guide**
- **Rationale**
- **It isn't important to document everything all at once**
- **Ok to just say TBD**
- **Iterative and evolutionary**
- **Text offers many samples of UML & informal notations**
- **Elements, behaviors and relationships are the same**

Before I conclude our discussion regarding views, I want to include a few points that may not be apparent. In my examples, I primarily covered the three main view types focusing on a few styles of each view type. I've done this to provide a few practical examples that will help you get started. One important note is that each of these diagrams is only a portion of what a view should contain. Each view begins with the diagram as the primary presentation, but this is but a portion of what each view must communicate to your stakeholders. Each view must include an Element catalog where each element identified in your diagram is described and whose interfaces and behaviors are notated. It must additionally include a Variability guide that describes the ability of the architecture to be tailored to suit the needs of the solution. And lastly, a Rationale section that describes why certain design choices were made, as well as to any design related information that might be useful. I've not provided examples of these as they're fairly self-explanatory and could be found in the text. Another thing I've stated before, but I want to reiterate, is that it isn't important to document everything all at once. Feel free to add sections that will be flushed out later. It's okay to just say TBD when you're not entirely sure about something. Early on in the class I said get comfortable with ambiguity; you'll encounter it often when designing in documenting solutions. Many things change in the course of a project's life cycle so expect it and give yourself permission to leave some things undefined. Remember, designing and documenting a solution is both an iterative and evolutionary process. It will take many iterations to reach completion and will no doubt evolve into something very different from what you envisioned early on in the project. Lastly, I'd like to comment on the notation style. I provided primarily informal hybrid style diagrams. I've done this because I find the informal notations much more intuitive than UML, but if your preference is

UML, then the text offers many samples of each of these styles using UML. Whether you choose UML or an informal notation, the elements, behaviors, and relationships are the same, and in most cases explicitly identified. This portion of the book was meant as an introduction to documentation practice. To further your education, I would encourage everyone taking this book to review the Views and Beyond approach outlined in Documenting Software Architecture: Views and Beyond. There are other approaches, but I personally have found this to be one of the more practical.

Summary

Well that's it for this module. We've covered quite a bit of material on how to design and communicate a solution to all your stakeholders.

- Design
    - Goals of software architecture & detailed design
    - How they are different
    - Who should perform them
    - Role of architecture in an agile world
    - Two fundamental approaches
    - Top-down
    - Bottom-up
- Architectural Design Process
    - Design considerations
    - Design process step by step
    - Prototypes
    - Architectural patterns

- When to use them

In the first half of this module, we covered Design by outlining the goals of software architecture and detailed design, discussing how they're different and who should perform them. We discussed the role of architecture in the agile world and how to apply the concepts we learned in the class when using agile methodologies. We also spent some time discussing the two fundamental approaches to architectural design: Top-down and Bottom-up. We covered the Architectural Design Process in detail, first by understanding design considerations and then by walking through the design process step by step. We also touched on Prototypes, Architectural patterns, and when to use them.

- Communicating the Solution
  - 3 main objectives
  - Documentation standards
- Views
  - 4+1 architectural view model
  - Views and beyond
- Views & Beyond applied
  - Module
  - Component-and-Connector
  - Allocation

In the second half of the module, we covered Communicating your Solution. We covered the 3 main objectives of architectural documentation and Documentation standards. We discussed Views and how they're utilized in the 4+1 architectural view and the Views and Beyond approach. Lastly, I provided some practical examples of how the Views and Beyond approach could be applied in the real world, showing examples

of Module, Component-and-Connector, and Allocation views.

www.ingramcontent.com/pod-product-compliance
Lightning Source LLC
Chambersburg PA
CBHW071117050326
40690CB00008B/1253